PREVIEWS OF COMING ATTRACTIONS

Sermons for Advent, Christmas and Epiphany
Cycle C First Lesson Texts

BY RON LAVIN

C.S.S Publishing Co., Inc.
Lima, Ohio

PREVIEWS OF COMING ATTRACTIONS

Copyright © 1991 by
The C.S.S. Publishing Company, Inc.
Lima, Ohio

All rights reserved. No part of this publication may be reproduced, stored in a retrieval system, or transmitted in any form or by any means, electronic, mechanical, photocopying, recording, or otherwise, without the prior permission of the publisher. Inquiries should be addressed to: The C.S.S. Publishing Company, Inc., 628 South Main Street, Lima, Ohio 45804.

Library of Congress Cataloging-in-Publication Data

Lavin, Ronald J.
    Previews of coming attractions : sermons for Advent, Christmas and Epiphany : cycle C first lesson texts / by Ron Lavin.
        p.   cm.
    Includes bibliographical references.
    ISBN 1-55673-317-8
    1. Advent sermons.   2. Christmas sermons.   3. Epiphany season—Sermons.   4. Jesus Christ—Transfiguration—Sermons.   5. Bible. O.T.—Sermons.   6. Sermons, American.   I. Title
BV40.L37   1991
252'.61—dc20
                                          90-25464
                                               CIP

9138 / ISBN 1-55673-317-8   PRINTED IN U.S.A.

Dedicated to my father, Harry Lavin,
who was baptized June 14, 1989,
while this book was being written.
He died January 27, 1991. Dedicated
also to our five grandchildren:
Lydia, Sarah and Heidi Wilkinson,
David and Peter Pflibsen.

Table Of Contents

Preface	7
Preview	9
In Appreciation	13
Advent 1 Previews Of Coming Attractions Jeremiah 33:14-16	15
Advent 2 Preparing The Way Malachi 3:1-4	21
Advent 3 Singing Along The Way Zephaniah 3:14-18	27
Advent 4 The Quest And The Question Of The Way Micah 5:2-4	33
The Nativity Of Our Lord Good News! Isaiah 52:7-10	37
Christmas 1 A Mother's Pride And Joy 1 Samuel 2:18-20, 26	43
Christmas 2 Mourning Turned To Joy Jeremiah 31:6-14	49
The Baptism Of Our Lord Anointed Isaiah 61:1-4	55

Epiphany 2 61
    From Inferiority To Fulfillment
    Isaiah 62:1-5

Epiphany 3 67
    The Water Gate And The Word Proclaimed
    Nehemiah 8:1-4a, 5-6, 8-10

Epiphany 4 73
    Dispelling Ministry Illusions
    Jeremiah 1:4-10

Epiphany 5 79
    Vision For Mission
    Isaiah 6:1-8

Epiphany 6 85
    Trusting In The Lord
    Jeremiah 17:5-10

Epiphany 7 89
    Faithful To The Lord
    Genesis 45:3-11, 15

Epiphany 8 95
    Believing The Living Word
    Isaiah 55:10-13

The Transfiguration Of Our Lord 101
    Transformed For The Great Awakening
    Exodus 34:29-35

Preface

What a rich resource to my life have been the Old Testament Bible stories that I learned at the feet of Dorothy Jones, my kindergarten Sunday school teacher at St. Paul's Lutheran Church in Greenville, Ohio. I want so much for the present and future generations to know the wealth of those Old Testament stories. Ron Lavin's book, *Previews Of Coming Attractions,* fills the bill.

These gospel-centered and grace-filled sermons are affirming of our lives. They are upbeat and positive, cleverly crafted, and written to be spoken and studied.

There is something very nice about this series of sermons based on Old Testament stories which helps us anticipate the future and enjoy our present situation. They bring insight to how we sinners are now and what we might envision for future times.

Ron Lavin is a story teller par excellence. He knows the art of narrative and illustration. The sermons are close to the ground and applicable to living in present times, yet they give us a vision of what God would like us to be and what our possibilities really are.

Typical of the personality of the author, there is punch and humor. There is pathos and delight in the telling of the many illustrations sprinkled through the proclamation.

One can sense the forward motion as the messages are read. It is as if the themes of long ago are furnishing the propellant to launch us into the future unafraid, much like those who lived the stories.

Throughout the entire collection of sermons is a basic Christian ingredient of evangelism. One senses a quiet passion for sharing this good news with anyone who will listen, not unlike that in the life and ministry of the author.

I am glad for *Previews Of Coming Attractions,* for it assures me that the stories that so instruct my own life and those I love and with whom I worship will be transmitted and applied to the lives of future generations as well.

To meet and minister with the author is to have a sneak preview of what is coming next in this book.

Dr. Jerry L. Schmalenberger
President, Pacific Lutheran Theological Seminary

Preview

When you go to the movies and see the coming attractions, you know what movies are coming to the theatre in the near future. You make decisions about whether or not you will see the movies you preview. When you read the Old Testament, you are also previewing what is coming.

What is coming? The Messiah. Many of the chapters in this book are about the announcement of the Anointed One, the Savior who is predicted and prophesied. The Old Testament prophets not only foretell Christ's coming but tell forth the meaning of the Messiah's entrance into the world. A case in point is Isaiah 9:6-7.

> *For to us a child is born, to us a son is given; and the government will be upon his shoulder, and his name will be called "Wonderful Counselor, Mighty God, everlasting Father, Prince of Peace." Of the increase of his government and of peace there will be no end, upon the throne of David, and over his kingdom, to establish it, and to uphold it with justice and with righteousness from this time forth and for evermore. The zeal of the Lord of hosts will do this.*

Another illustration of prophetic forth-telling as well as foretelling is Micah 5:2:

> *But you, O Bethlehem Ephrathah, who are little to be among the clans of Judah, from you shall come forth for me one who is to be ruler . . .*

Both passages foretell who is coming and tell forth what the Messiah will do, namely, rule with power. These Old Testament passages are previews of the coming attractions called the reign of God.

What is coming? The reign of God, which is frequently called the kingdom of God, is coming in its fullness in the person of the Messiah. Christmas and Easter, the two great Christian festivals, are examples of the reign of God breaking into history in the incarnation and the resurrection of the Messiah.

What is coming? Christmas is coming. Are we ready? Advent prepares us for the celebration of Christmas. What is coming? Easter! Epiphany helps to prepare us for Lent which in turn prepares us for Easter. All of these seasons are previews of coming attractions — Christmas and Easter, which in turn point beyond themselves to the ultimate reign of the ultimate One.

What is coming? The Messiah's ministry is coming. Isaiah 40:1-5 and Isaiah 61:1-6 predict this coming attraction.

> *Comfort, comfort, my people, says your God. Speak tenderly to Jerusalem and cry to her that her warfare is ended, that her iniquity is pardoned, that she has received from the Lord's hand double for all her sins. A voice cries: "In the wilderness prepare the way of the Lord, make straight in the desert a highway for our God. Every valley shall be lifted up, and every mountain and hill be made low and uneven ground shall become level, and the rough places a plain. And the glory of the Lord shall be revealed, and all flesh shall see it together, for the mouth of the Lord has spoken."*

> *The Spirit of the Lord God is upon me, because the Lord has anointed me to bring good tidings to the afflicted; he has sent me to bind up the brokenhearted, to proclaim liberty to the captives, and the opening of the prison to those who are bound; to proclaim the year of the Lord's favor, and the day of vengeance of our God; to comfort all who mourn; to grant to those who mourn in Zion — to give them a garland instead of ashes, the oil of gladness instead of mourning, the mantle of praise instead of a faint spirit; that they may be called oaks of righteousness, the planting of the Lord that he may be glorified . . . men shall speak of you as the ministers of our God; you shall eat the wealth of the nations, and in their riches you shall glory.*

What is coming? The ministry of the Messiah results in ministries among the people of God: "Men shall speak of you as ministers of our God." All of this is made possible by the surprising end of the surprising ministry of Jesus and his chosen 12: crucifixion and death.

What is coming? The death of the Messiah, the method for more fully ushering in the kingdom of God predicted in Isaiah 53:3-7:

> *He was despised and rejected by men; a man of sorrows, and acquainted with grief; and as one from whom men hide their faces he was despised, and we esteemed him not. Surely he has borne our griefs and carried our sorrows; yet we esteemed him stricken, smitten by God, and afflicted. But he was wounded for our transgressions, he was bruised for our iniquities; upon him was the chastisement that made us whole, and with his stripes we are healed. All we like sheep have gone astray; we have turned everyone to his own way; and the Lord has laid on him the iniquity of us all. He was oppressed, and he was afflicted, yet he opened not his mouth; like a lamb that is led to slaughter, and like a sheep that before its shearers is dumb, so he opened not his mouth.*

What is coming? The Messiah's cruel death is coming. Isaiah 53 gives us a preview of coming attractions.

This looks like a horror movie, a tragedy of demonic proportions. But what is actually coming is a comedy, not of Laurel and Hardy variety, but a divine comedy, a surprising upturn in the midst of sorrow and sadness.

What's coming? Easter's victory and after it, Pentecost's power and after it, Ascension's foretaste of the end of time when Jesus shall reign forever and ever and all shall acknowledge the Lord. Paul says, "Every knee shall bow . . . and every tongue confess that Jesus Christ is Lord, to the glory of God the Father (Philippians 2:10-11)."

What is coming? The end of the world. The kingdom or full reign of God is coming at the end of time. The date is unknown. The timing of this coming is like a thief in the night.

The full reign of God will come suddenly, when we least expect it. In the Old Testament (and the New Testament) the kingdom of God is a coming attraction with a serendipity beyond our wildest dreams. Are we ready? Here and now we have a foretaste. Are we tasting it? Foretaste and readiness are twin themes of this book about preparation for the ultimate reign of God.

This book is a series of expositions of Old Testament texts for the Advent, Christmas, Epiphany and Transfiguration. The order of the chapters is not chronological. The order of the chapters is determined by how these Old Testament texts fit into the church year from Advent through Transfiguration. "Are we ready?" is the unwritten question throughout the book.

This book, as a preview of coming attractions, is intended to help people make choices about the present and the future. While we have no choice about the reality and the timing of the end of the world or the end of our own lives, we do have choices about what we will watch, what we will hear, what we will do and what will get our attention and devotion. This book is intended to help with these choices. The Old Testament helps with these choices.

The Old Testament is neglected. Christians don't read it enough. Hopefully this book will be an encouragement to look at Old Testament previews of coming attractions and thus better understand the premiere show in the New Testament, which itself is a preview of the ultimate reign of God. The purpose of this book is to make us all more aware that God is coming. The method of this book is to take Old Testament texts as proleptics of what is coming in the church year, the first appearing of the Messiah and the second coming of the Messiah at the end of time.

In Appreciation

Special thanks are given to Jewel Becsi, Madeline Peterson, Jo Capps, and Suzy Hickok who typed this material. Ruth Hancock, my assistant, and Edythe Ellig served as editors for this book. Their encouragement, as well as their sharp eyes for errors, made this a better work.

Special appreciation is expressed to the leaders and staff at Our Saviour's Lutheran Church in Tucson who provided space for the writing as well as partnership for the ministry in Tucson. Without the congregational context, this book would have been impossible.

Joyce, my wife, is always an encourager. She comes from the School of St. Barnabas, the great companion and partner of St. Paul. St. Barnabas ("Uncle Barney") founded a movement called "The Encouragers" in the first century. That movement continues on in our day. I am blessed with friends and family who belong to that movement.

Note that I have used the following abbreviated forms of the various Bible references. RSV - Revised Standard Version; TEV - Today's English Version; J B Phillips - J B Phillips paraphrase; JB - Jerusalem Bible; NAB - New American Bible.

Advent 1
Jeremiah 33:14-16

Previews Of Coming Attractions

What comes to your mind when I say the word "forecasting"? The weather man? The predictor of tomorrow's heat, cold, rain, humidity? Probably so.

In the Bible, the forecaster is God's prophet. He tells us what is going to happen in the future based on the reality of the present. True prophecy involves both forth-telling and foretelling. Jeremiah tells forth and foretells by giving us previews of coming attractions.

What comes to your mind when I say, "previews of coming attractions"? Perhaps you think of movie previews wherein you get enticing scenes of a forthcoming movie which makes you want to see it. The previews in Jeremiah are two-fold: (1) previews of destruction we would just as soon avoid, and (2) previews of reconstruction which we embrace when we know that the destruction is unavoidable and that our future hope lies in God's action of redeeming and reforming his people.

Jeremiah 33:14-16 is a redeeming and reforming passage in the prophecy of Jeremiah, but we must consider the context of destruction before we can appreciate the reconstruction. Gloom precedes glory in this forecast.

The Destruction

Jeremiah was a man of great inner conflict, knowing he must speak for God, but feeling great inadequacy and reluctance. He was called by Yahweh when he was just a teenager. He protested, "I am only a youth (Jeremiah 1:6)," but the Lord replied, "Be not afraid of them, for I am with you to deliver you . . . . Then the Lord put forth his hand and touched my mouth; and the Lord said to me, 'Behold I have put my words in your mouth' (Jeremiah 1:8-10)."

Jeremiah was also a God-driven man, fearlessly denouncing the idolatry of his day, perpetual backsliding (Jeremiah 8:5) and religious laxity, and inordinate self-centeredness.[1] He warned of the impending disaster that would come from the sins of the people. This lonely and sensitive young man began to speak for Yahweh fearlessly and dramatically. Fearlessly, Jeremiah denounced the false idols of wisdom, human strength, and money:

> *Let not the wise man glory in his wisdom, let not the mighty man glory in his might, let not the rich man glory in his riches, but let him who glories glory in this, that he understands and knows me, that I am the Lord who practices kindness, justice, and righteousness in the earth; for in these things I delight, says the Lord.*
> — Jeremiah 9:23-24, RSV

Jeremiah's fearless criticisms brought him continual trouble with the secular and religious authorities. One sabbath day, the prophet planted himself in front of the temple and sternly predicted its downfall if the people did not mend their ways:

> *Will you steal, murder, commit adultery, swear falsely, burn incense to Baal, and go after other gods that you have not known and then come and stand before me in this house, which is called by my name and say "We are delivered!" only to go on doing all these abominations?*
> — Jeremiah 7:9-10

Jeremiah fearlessly spoke of the stiff-necked people who refused to hear the word of the Lord (Jeremiah 19:15). With urgency he pleaded for repentance. He predicted, "This whole land shall become a ruin and a waste, and these nations shall serve the king of Babylon seventy years (Jeremiah 25:11)." He also predicted the death of the impious king, Jehoiakim.

> *With the burial of an ass he shall be buried, dragged and cast forth beyond the gates of Jerusalem.*
> — Jeremiah 22:19

In the valley of Hinnom, Jeremiah dramatically smashed a piece of pottery saying,

> *Thus says the Lord of hosts: So will I break this people and this city as one breaks a potter's vessel, so it can never be mended.* — Jeremiah 19:11

Dramatically, Jeremiah went about Jerusalem with a wooden yoke on his neck, symbolizing the bondage to the Babylonians which was forthcoming. The Babylonians sacked the faithless city in 587 B.C., as Jeremiah predicted.

Just before the destruction of Jerusalem, Jeremiah dramatically purchased land to symbolize the promise that the people would return after exile. This land purchase, plus many of Jeremiah's words about genuine comfort and a new covenant, put us in touch with the compassionate side of this fiery prophet. Jeremiah's prediction of the coming Messiah is even greater evidence of this compassion in the prophet and in Yahweh.

Thus we've gone full circle back to the place where we began, the Messianic prophecy of Jeremiah 33:14-16 that "a righteous Branch will spring forth for David." Jeremiah tells forth about the judgment of God in the Babylonian captivity; he also foretells of the release from captivity in the coming Messiah.

Reconstruction

The "righteous Branch springing forth for David" means an ideal ruler of the Davidic law who will guide the destiny of the people of God.

Jeremiah 23:5-6 says:

> Behold, the days are coming, says the Lord when I will raise up for David a righteous Branch, and he shall reign as king and deal wisely, and shall execute justice and righteousness in the land. In his days Judah will be saved, and Israel will dwell securely. And this is the name by which he will be called: "The Lord is our righteousness."

This ideal ruler will usher in the new covenant of the law in the hearts of the people (Jeremiah 31:31-34) wherein Yahweh will show mercy on sinners, "forgiving their iniquity and remembering their sin no more." "I will turn their mourning into joy, I will comfort them, and give them gladness for sorrow (Jeremiah 31:13)." This new covenant time of forgiveness and mercy is fulfilled in Jesus, the son of Mary, in the line of David.

Jesus is the Righteous One. The book of Hebrews says, Jesus was "tempted as we are, yet without sinning (Hebrews 4:15)." Jesus entered into the flesh (the incarnation) and identified with us as sinners. "He became sin," Paul says. Yet, Jesus himself did not sin. He is the Righteous One, the One and only One who did no wrong.

Jesus knows who we are as sinners because he comes to where we sin. No place is too dirty, too ugly, too unrighteous for this Righteous One to enter. Jesus knows our every weakness; thus he loves us into understanding our need to change. Reconstruction of our personalities takes place through the love of the Righteous One.

A story is told about a woman shopping in a drug store in a large eastern city. She noticed a small boy taking jars from the counter and playing with them on the floor. A clerk also noticed him, and ordered him to stop. The child looked up, bewildered. He couldn't understand what the clerk was saying. Suddenly the woman realized what the clerk did not; the boy was mentally retarded. In a moment he began playing with the items again. Now the clerk started shouting, threatening the child with a loud, angry voice.

Just then a girl about seven or eight years old came around the end of the counter. She sized up the situation with a glance. And then she acted. Running over to the boy, she dropped to her knees, put her arm around him, and began whispering softly. Now the child understood. Slowly and carefully he began replacing the items on the shelf.

Then the girl stood and turned to the clerk. Her voice was still calm and soft. "He doesn't understand when you talk that way," she said. "He understands me — because I put love into him."[2]

In Jeremiah we have a loving prophet, one who reveals the way it really is (forth-telling) and the way it will be (foretelling). In a way it is frightening to face the truth with no illusions, yet it is comforting, too, especially because we, with Jeremiah, hear the good news, "I am with you," as well as the bad news, "Destruction will surely come on all sin."

In Jeremiah we have previews of coming attractions — both destruction and reconstruction. We also have a forecasting of the greatest news of all: the Savior, the righteous Branch of David, will love us into the changes we need to make.

---

1. Ron Lavin, *Hey Mom Look at Me,* C.S.S. Publishers, Lima, Ohio, 1973.
2. Mason, *Emphasis* Magazine, C.S.S Publishers, Lima, Ohio, October, 1988, page 35.

Advent 2
Malachi 3:1-4
Preparing The Way

Frank kept the strangest of Christmas lists. He called it "My Refinement List." He first made one out when he was 45 years old. He worked at it faithfully for 29 years. He was 74 and a grandfather. In all that time it had remained a secret, but now his youngest grandchild, with the piece of paper clutched in hand, looked Frank dead in the eye, and said, "What's this?"

"A special Christmas list," answered Frank, a bit vaguely.

"Is it what you want?" asked the boy.

"It's not that kind of a list," answered Frank.

"Is it what you're going to give other people?" the boy asked, wishing he could read.

"Well, no, it's not that kind of a list either." Then groping for words to explain something he felt was important and wanted to pass on, Frank lifted the boy into his lap. "A few weeks before Christmas I just write down the things I'd like God to help me get rid of, like selfishness, or being impatient with your grandmother, or wanting too many things for myself. I figure the more I get rid of things like that, the more I'll be able to rejoice in the good things God gives us all."[1]

Grandpa Frank's list is a way of preparing for God's coming. This Advent list provided Frank with a way to do a spiritual housecleaning for a special guest. Frank's special preparation had to do with selfishness, impatience and inordinately desiring things. That's a special kind of preparing the way for the advent of the Lord. Do any of these maladies make your refinement list?

It is that kind of preparation which Malachi and John the Baptist (the messenger of Malachi 3:1) have in mind as they think of the coming of God. Both of these prophets, one in the Old Testament and one in the New Testament, speak of cleansing of sin in preparation for the coming of the Lord. Both are messengers of Yahweh, pointing to one greater than themselves who is on his way and is about to arrive.

If God were on his way to your house, what clean-up would you want to do? Frank had his list; Malachi had his list; John the Baptist had his list; and we should have our lists.

Malachi's List

Malachi[2] was the last of the minor prophets from the fifth century B.C. As we study the last book of the Old Testament which bears his name, three areas of clean-up jump out at us. Malachi cries out for faithfulness in worship, morality and speech. The three human maladies here addressed are (1) religious slackness, (2) moral erosion and (3) the complaining of the people.

First of all, due to the economic depression of the times, the people of God became slack in their worship practices. "Why go to temple?" they asked. "Why pray?" they asked. "Yahweh doesn't care for us. Why should we care about him and his laws?" Lean harvests, droughts, and locusts swarming on crops resulted in most of the people staying away from worship services. The people also stopped giving their tithes and offerings and were thus robbing God (Malachi 3:8-12). It isn't much different today. The biggest reason for faithlessness in worship and giving to the Lord's work is personal crises. Cheating God by not giving offerings often comes from not coping with personal crises through faith. Do any of these areas make your refinement list?

Secondly, personal crises can also produce immorality. Five sins of immorality are listed in Malachi 3:5: (1) the practice of magic (astrology); (2) adultery (sexual deviations); (3) lying (telling distortions or half-truths and hurting people with words); (4) cheating (especially cheating one's employees); and (5) not helping widows, orphans and foreigners (those with special needs or of a different skin, color and national background than us). Do any of these five maladies make your refinement list? Correcting immorality is a major way of preparing to meet God. Looking at our behavior in the light of the ten commandments is a good way to get ready for the special visitor who is coming.

Malachi, speaking for Yahweh, says, "You, like your ancestors before you, have turned away from my laws and have not kept them (Malachi 3:7, TEV)." Does breaking the commandments of God make your refinement list?

Thirdly, let's look at complaining against God. Is murmuring a problem for you? Is cynicism on your sin list? How about complaining against God?

"Your words have been stout against me, says the Lord (Malachi 3:13, RSV)." The TEV puts it this way: "You have said terrible things about me," says the Lord. "But you ask, 'What have we said about you?' You have said, 'It is useless to serve God. What's the use of doing what he says or of trying to show the Lord Almighty that we are sorry for what we have done? As we see it, proud people are the ones who are happy. Evil men not only prosper, but they test God's patience with their evil deeds and get away with it' (Malachi 3:13-15, TEV)."

Murmuring against God may very well be on our Advent preparation lists. Getting ready for God's coming means turning away from self-centered complaints. That's not an easy task, but we don't have to do it by some super-human effort. The task of cleaning up our complaints and other sins is the work of the Holy Spirit. In other words, the cleanup task we are told to do is really the work of God with which we just cooperate. God is at work in our lives helping us to do what needs to be done to prepare for his coming. If we just appropriate what has already been given, we can see murmuring for what it really is: a sin against our Lord.

How is this possible? Malachi says God works like a refiner and a fuller to make us ready for his arrival. A refiner's fire is very hot, so hot that metallic substances are melted and purified. In God's foundry people are purified by fire. Repentance isn't easy, but it is needed.

In God's fullers' field people are cleansed. Repentance is like clothing being scrubbed and rubbed clean in the fullers' field outside the walls of Jerusalem. A fuller is one who cleans and whitens cloth. The specific reference in our text is to the coarse soap which a fuller must use to do his job. Oil and grease must go. The clothing must be steeped in soapy water and trodden (beaten) clean.

Malachi is not done with us as he speaks of the harsh ways of the fiery furnace and the fullers' soap. He also speaks to us of God's sending of the prophet Elijah. "Behold, I will send you Elijah the prophet before the great and terrible day of the Lord comes. And he will turn the hearts of fathers to their children, and the hearts of children to their fathers, lest I come and smite the land with a curse (Malachi 4:5-6)."

John's List

John the Baptist is that Elijah who fulfills Malachi's prophecy. Jesus himself says so: "He (John) is Elijah who is to come (Matthew 11:14)[3]."

John comes as a fiery prophet in the wilderness, seeking to cleanse the lives of his listeners, thus fulfilling Malachi's words about fire refining and fullers' soap. John speaks of preparing the way of the Lord in three ways, (1) straightening crooked paths and roads, (2) by raising valleys, and (3) by lowering mountains (Luke 3:1-6), thus fulfilling Isaiah's prophecy of the coming Messiah.

First of all, your Advent list might include straightening out some pathway which is crooked. Crooked means distorted, dishonest or deformed. "You brood of vipors," John called some of the people who came to see him at the Jordan River, "who told you that you could escape from God's punishment (Luke 3:7)?" These snakes were the unrepentant sinners who refused to acknowledge their distorted, dishonest and deformed ways.

Secondly, raising valleys is different than straightening crooked places. The symbolic meaning of this highway construction imagery is that many people are kept from proper preparation for meeting God by their depression and feelings of inferiority. "God will raise up valleys," John says. God seeks to help the lowly by reconstructing their minds. The afflicted will be raised and comforted. One man put it this way: "The purpose of preaching is to comfort the afflicted and afflict the comfortable." Valleys are raised. Mountains are lowered.

Thirdly, the mountains and hills of this prophecy are those elements of pride which keep us from repentance. Repentance is John's ultimate theme. *Metanoia,* the Greek word we translate as repentance, means turning around or turning back to God. That's the most important item on our refinement list.

A dear friend, Dr. Vic Pearson, a retired Lutheran theologian, died when he was 96 years old. While receiving private communion shortly before his death, Vic listened intently to the confessional service which precedes the communion. As we shared our confession of sins, he interrupted, "Oh, yes, Pastor. How true that is!" It isn't that he had sinned so terribly by actions at the nursing home where he lived. Vic just knew that all of us are "turned in on self," as Luther described sin.

"Selfishness, impatience and materialism are all on my list," grandfather Frank said to his grandson. Religious slackness, moral erosion and complaining were on Malachi's list. Crookedness, inferiority and pride made John's list. What items belong on our lists that we may be made ready for the coming of our special guest? God is coming!

---

1. Stephen V. Daughty *Emphasis* magazine, C.S.S. Publishers, Lima, Ohio, December 1988, page 6.

2. Malachi means messenger. We do not know whether this was a man named Malachi or an unknown person who was God's messenger.

3. Also see Mark 9:12-13 and Luke 1:17.

Advent 3
Zephaniah 3:14-18

Singing Along The Way

In the time of John the Baptist, most of the people were not getting the point. There was political corruption with Herod, religious corruption with Annas and Caiaphas, the high priests, and confusion among the general populace. It was the time right before the Messiah would appear, so John the Baptist and a small remnant of followers echoed prophetic words at the Jordan River. To the superficially interested who heard his preaching, John warned, "You brood of vipers (Luke 3:7, J B Phillips)." "You snakes, who told you that you could escape from the punishment that God is about to send (Luke 3:7, TEV)?" Interestingly, from this "hell, fire and damnation" preaching of John the Baptist, "the peoples' hopes began to rise" (Luke 3:15, TEV) or as the Jerusalem Bible puts it, "a feeling of expectancy had grown that John might be the Messiah . . . ." "Me?" John asked.

"I'm not even worthy to untie the shoelace of the Messiah (Paraphrase of Luke 3:16)."

What does this have to do with our text from Zephaniah? Like John, Zephaniah was a prophet who told the truth with power, even though this message flew in the face of secular and religious authorities. Like John's message, the message of Zephaniah began to make some peoples' hopes and expectations rise. Thus we hear the rejoicing of the remnant, the few who were left to respond positively to the word of God:

> *Sing aloud, O Daughter of Zion;*
> *shout, O Israel!*
> *Rejoice and exult with all your heart,*
> *O Daughter of Jerusalem!*
> — Zephaniah 3:14

Before we look further at this rejoicing of the remnant, let us look at the situation in Zephaniah's day.

The Situation

The time was the seventh century B.C. in Judah. Zephaniah, about whom we know precious little, was a contemporary of Jeremiah. The people were in the throes of idolatry. King Josiah, a man of God, was trying to restore the worship of the one true God. While meeting with outward success, the hearts of the people were still loyal to man-made gods. The poor and the afflicted were neglected under the philosophy "each man for himself." Only a small band of real believers could be found. They were called, "the remnant."

This remnant concept goes back to the time of Moses. The majority of the people missed the point and sought idols of the one true God. Only a dedicated minority along with Moses carried the true message of Yahweh.

The concept of the remnant was sharpened among the prophets. The prophets said that even though most of the people miss the message, God will keep for himself a dedicated minority of people who will keep the truth alive from generation to generation. Nehemiah speaks of a remnant of the captivity (Nehemiah 1:3). Isaiah speaks of a small remnant left (Isaiah 1:9; 11:11) ". . . who shall travel the highway of our God (Isaiah 11:16)." This remnant "shall be very small and weak (Isaiah 16:14)." Jeremiah says, "I will gather a remnant of my flock (Jeremiah 23:3)." "The Lord will save this remnant of Israel (Jeremiah 31:7)." "Hear the Lord, ye remnant of Judah (Jeremiah 42:15)." Zephaniah also promulgated the concept of the remnant.

"This remnant shall not do iniquity," Zephaniah cried (3:13). "The remnant shall possess the land (2:9)." Those few who are left, the remnant, shall not do wrong, nor utter lies, nor utter deceitful words; they shall not be afraid (3:13). Zephaniah also said that this remnant shall sing and rejoice. That brings us back to chapter three, verse 14 of the prophecy of Zephaniah.

The Prescription

The prescription for holding onto the truth when everyone else wants to care nothing for it is focusing on Yahweh instead of the idolatrous behavior of the people. One of the ways to do that, says the prophet Zephaniah, is to sing songs to and about Yahweh. In the melody and the words of these "Songs of Zion" is the hope of staying loyal when the majority of the people are caught in chaos.

"Sing aloud, O Daughter of Zion (Zephaniah 3:14)."

This singing is not in harmony with the world's song. The world is singing a very different tune than the remnant sings. The remnant sings songs to the Lord.

One of our members recently asked me, "Is it just me? Maybe I'm out of sync with what's happening. Everyone, including my own relatives is committing immoral acts of sex outside of marriage and telling me that it is not a sin. Maybe I'm crazy and they are all right." This member was seeking to remain part of the remnant. How shall we do that? Sing the songs of Zion.

William Barclay, the New Testament scholar, in his book *Ethics in a Permissive Society* says that when he came out of seminary the divisive questions were doctrinal, but almost all Christians agreed on the difference between right and wrong. In our time of ethical relativism, people do as they please and rationalize their behavior. Yet, the ethics of the Bible are as valid today as ever. Biblical ethics deal with unchangeable truths. Barclay is speaking of the unchangeable God in the midst of a changeable and fickle people. Barclay speaks of carrying on the remnant song in our time. After 1950 years of Christian tradition many have decided that "everyone for himself" is the proper tune. How shall we keep from being drawn into permissiveness? "Sing the songs of Zion . . .," Zephaniah advises.

"Sing, aloud, O Daughter of Zion." Hang in there by focusing on God and his ways, even if you have to stand all alone for the truth. Singing can help us focus on God and avoid the alluring songs of the world which are calling us to death and destruction. The remnants' songs can keep God's people from going the way of all flesh. The remnants' song, "Rejoice and exult," gives glory to God.

Johann Sebastian Bach wrote at the top of each of his manuscripts "JJ" which stood for "Jesus Juva," or "Jesus help me." At the end of each manuscript Bach wrote "SDG" which stood for "solo dei gloria," or "to God alone the praise." Bach is a part of the remnant focusing on the glory of God instead of the glory of humankind. The song of the remnant is "Rejoice with all your heart, O daughter of Jerusalem." Many people, the majority, live in this world as if there is no other. What a surprise there will be when the day of the Lord comes. Bach gives us a prayer and a question to use before the day of the Lord. The prayer is "Jesus help me." The question is "Does it glorify God?"

We all need this reminder for ethical living. I needed the reminder recently. I had called a mortgage company long distance to get some information. An answering machine, not a person, greeted me and gave me seven options. The first six options had to do with pushing certain buttons on my touch-tone phone for specific departments. I don't have a touch-tone phone. I have a dial phone. That was the seventh option. "An operator will come on the line if you don't have a touch-tone phone," the automatic machine said. I finally got the department I thought I needed, but the person I talked to couldn't help me. She put me on hold. I was doing a slow burn.

This was a long distance call! I had been on the phone for 15 minutes and I had not yet talked to anyone to whom I could even address my questions, much less get answers. My patience was to be tried much further when someone finally picked up the phone and informed me that the receptionist had connected me to the wrong department.

When I reached the right department, I was switched back and forth between two clerks who couldn't help me. Finally, one of the clerks said, "You will have to talk to our supervisor about that problem, sir." "Fine," I said crisply, "but please do it promptly. This is long distance and I have been on the phone for 45 minutes and have gotten no answers."

"Hum," went the phone. She had put me on hold for what seemed like the hundredth time. I had a cold which made me even more irritated. I was at the end of my rope — angry, disgusted, and stressed to what I thought was the limit. I was beginning to forget the reason I had phoned. Suddenly out of the background from the "hold" position of the telephone system of this mammoth mortgage corporation came some music. This was the ultimate insult. They were trying to calm an irate customer with "elevator music." Only it wasn't "elevator music." It was a Christmas carol. I listened as a secular mortgage company telephone system played: "Silent night, Holy night. All is calm; all is bright."

I was laughing by the time the supervisor came to the phone. Music centered in God can do that. It can be a reminder of who you are. My sin of impatience became a laughing matter in the light of the coming Messiah. By the way, the supervisor could not answer my questions, but she told me that I could call her back.

Music can soothe the savage beast in all of us. God-centered music can keep us close to God when we reach the breaking point.

A gospel musician was away from home singing and inspiring people with his music. The phone rang. It was for him. The news was bad. His wife who was pregnant had lost the baby. "The baby is dead," he was told. That's staggering news. He started for home. A few days later his wife died.

He had sung the gospel of comfort to many, but he could not find comfort anywhere. Friends and relatives tried in vain to help him with his grief, but it was all to no avail. He went to God in prayer . . . and expressed his need in music. From his sorrow, Thomas A. Dorsey wrote the spiritual:

Precious Lord, take my hand
Lead me on, let me stand;
I am tired, I am weak, I am worn.

> *Through the storm, through the night,*
> *Lead me on to the light.*
> *Take my hand, precious Lord,*
> *Lead me home.*

Music centered in God can calm the violent darkness in all of us. Such music is the voice of one crying in the wilderness, "Through the storm, through the light, Lead me on to the light . . ."

John the Baptist along with Zephaniah and all the prophets were voices crying in the wilderness, "Prepare ye the way of the Lord."

John and Zephaniah are vivid reminders of the remnant seeking the glory of God in everything. Our hopes and expectations can rise above the maddening crowd: "Precious Lord, take my hand, lead me on, let me stand."

> *Sing aloud, O Daughter of Zion;*
> *Shout, O Israel!*
> *Rejoice and exult with all your heart,*
> *O Daughter of Jerusalem.*

Advent 4
Micah 5:2-4

The Quest And The Question Of The Way

Life is a quest. For some, life is a quest for power. These people spend their waking hours planning and scheming to gain power over others. Perhaps Washington, D.C. is the symbolic city for those whose question is "How can I gain power over others?"

For some, life is a quest for money. They spend their time and energies getting things and spending money. Materialism is their God. Perhaps Las Vegas is the symbolic city most often associated with "glitz" and gaining or losing huge sums of money.

For some, the glory of winning is their quest. In sports, it has been said, "winning isn't everything; it is the only thing." In business, competition can run rampant and ruthless to such a degree that winning is the only thing. People can get crushed in the process. Perhaps New York is the city which symbolizes winning and glory at any price in the minds of most people.

Bethlehem is the city for those whose quest is God. Beneath all other quests is this seeking to know and follow our creator. All other quests are idolatrous thrusts coming from the hidden drive God put into every human heart — to return to him. In terms of a small American town, many nominations might be made to help us see the lowliness of the city of Our Savior. For me, Podunk, Iowa, and Elbow Lake, Minnesota, come to mind. Can anything good come from Bethlehem, Podunk or Elbow Lake? I don't know about the other two, but the son of God came from Bethlehem. That's the answer given by the prophet Micah to the question about the ultimate ruler of the universe. "Bethlehem . . . you are one of the smallest towns . . . but out of you I will bring a ruler of Israel (Micah 5:2, TEV)." The implied question of this Word from God about the little town of Bethlehem is "Will we align ourselves with the lowly King from this obscure place?"

The Quest

Rulers come and go. Power passes. Riches and things rot and rust. Glory fades. We speak here of the ultimate quest for the only one for whom power, riches and glory are an understatement. Unexpectedly, in the Bible, lowliness is often associated with this ultimate quest for God who alone has lasting power, riches and glory. The lowly are exalted.

The exaltation of the lowly is certainly the theme of Micah's prophecy. Greed and avarice ruled like a monarch in the hearts of the nobles, the priests and the false prophets in the eighth century B.C. in Jerusalem where Micah lived. This lowly farmer-prophet promulgated the theme of exalting the lowly — the poor, the homeless and the exploited. The shrewd schemes and unscrupulous business practices of the rich and powerful resulted in the poor getting poorer. Micah called people back to the quest for God.

From the little town of Moresheth, 30 miles southwest of Jerusalem, came a man of God with a message from God. He was a poor farm boy from a small town. "Who do you think you are telling us what to do?" the power brokers of the city asked Micah. "What makes you so sure that you know the will of God?" they queried. Abhorring greed and cruel oppression, this farm boy-prophet of high, holy, moral earnestness, indignantly confronted the deceit and cruelty he uncovered in Jerusalem. "The will of God is on the side of the oppressed people," Micah said.

If you want to know who speaks for God, one of the best questions you can raise is, "Who speaks for the people, especially the little people who cannot speak for themselves?" Micah spoke for the speechless poor of Jerusalem.

One of the most famous passages in the writings of Micah is about the ultimate quest to know and do the will of God:

He (God) has showed you, O man,
What is good;
And what does the Lord require of you
But to do justice and to love kindness
And to walk humbly with your God?
— Micah 6:8, RSV

Justice, kindness and reverence are the three elements in the humble quest to know God and to be godly. Justice, kindness and reverence are the signs of God, so actually they are the signs of the true people of God. Justice, kindness and reverence are also the signs of the One who comes from the little town of Bethlehem.

Bethlehem, you are one of the smallest towns . . .
But out of you I will bring a ruler . . .
— Micah 5:2, TEV

"Do you really mean that you expect us to believe that we can find our ruler in Bethlehem?" "Yes," said Micah. "The quest for God has its fulfillment there." The quest for God is really a quest of God. God seeks us; only then do we seek God. The incarnation of the Son of God comes in a lowly town in the womb of a lowly maiden named Mary.

The Question

"Surely," some power-broker in Jerusalem said about Micah, "can anything good come out of Moresheth?" "Surely," some powerful and wealthy temple priest asked, "can anything good come out of Bethlehem?" We know that when Jesus' family fled Bethlehem, the town of great King David, because of Herod's slaughter of the innocent children, and went to Egypt for a time and then to Nazareth, another lowly place, that people raised the question, "Can anything good come out of Nazareth (John 1:46)?" Those are interesting questions about lowly towns and lowly people. Another lowly person raises another question.

Lowly Mary, the mother of Jesus, raises the ultimate question about the quest for God.

> *My soul magnifies the Lord,*
> *and my spirit rejoices in God my Savior,*
> *for He has regarded the lowly estate of his handmaiden.*
> *For behold, henceforth all generations will call me blessed;*
> *for he who is mighty has done great things for me,*
> *and holy is his name.*
> *And his mercy is on those who fear him*
> *from generation to generation.*
> *He has shown strength with his arm,*
> *he has scattered the proud in the imagination of their hearts,*
> *he has put down the mighty from their thrones,*
> *and exalted those of low degree;*
> *he has filled the hungry with good things,*
> *and the rich he has sent empty away,*
> *He has helped his servant Israel,*
> *in remembrance of his mercy,*
> *as he spoke to our fathers,*
> *to Abraham and to his posterity forever.*
> — Luke 1:46-55, RSV

Mary thus raises the ultimate question of God: "With whom will you and I align ourselves?" Will we join up with the powers of this world which are fading, with the riches of this world which are rotting and rusting, with the glory of this world which is going nowhere? Or will we align ourselves with the power, the riches, and the glory of God, which has put us on the ultimate winning side?

The Nativity Of Our Lord
Isaiah 52:7-10

Good News!

From your childhood, think of some good news which came to you suddenly. Maybe it was the announcement of a new baby in the family, or a new puppy. Maybe it was the announcement of a vacation or your first trip to Disneyland. Get in touch with the feeling of good news. That's especially helpful when there is so much bad news around.

We certainly hear enough bad news these days. Newspapers, television, and radio bombard us daily with news like: "Pam Am Jet Down;" "258 People Killed;" "Bomb Suspected;" "1,000s Of Homeless Sleep In The Streets;" and "Kadafy Builds Chemical Warfare Plant."

We begin to wonder if there is any good news anywhere. The people of God in Babylonian exiled in the sixth century B.C. wondered the same thing. They were in bondage to the Babylonians. They were surrounded by war and warriors. They heard bad news everywhere. There was little hope anywhere. Then a messenger running across the mountains broke in with good news: ". . . The Lord will return to Zion . . . The Lord will use his holy power; he will save his people, and all the world will see it (Isaiah 52:8-10, TEV)." This messenger said: "We are going to be released. We are going back to Zion. After 70 years of captivity, we are going home." That was good news! The announcement of the return of the Jewish exiles from Babylon to Jerusalem is the historical context of this Word from God.

Can people come home to God like the Jews came home to Jerusalem? How can this good news be translated for our day?

Paul Translated The Good News

Paul, the apostle, made the direct connection with the good news of return for his day. In Romans 10, he quotes Isaiah 52 and says that we Christians are the messengers of the good news of Christ.

> "... *Everyone who calls on the name of the Lord will be saved." But how can they call to him, if they have not believed? And how can they believe, if they have not heard the message? And how can they hear, if the message is not proclaimed? And how can the message be proclaimed, if the messengers are not sent out? As the Scripture says, "How wonderful is the coming of those who bring good news!" But they have not all accepted the Good News. Isaiah himself said, "Lord, who believed our message?" So then, faith comes from hearing the message, and the message comes through preaching Christ.* — Romans 10:13-17, TEV

In other words, Paul believes that Isaiah 52:7-10 should inspire Christians to get out and proclaim the good news of Christ's coming. Paul centers everything in Christ. He says, "... the message comes through preaching Christ."

If only unbelievers and borderline believers could see Christ, wouldn't they be released? Wouldn't they come home to God and home to the church? Christ said, "Come unto me." Christ invites us to come home to God.

Rosie, a 34-year-old woman, was miserable in her unbelief. She had been a Christian as a child, but she was reared in an oppressive church which had so many rules and regulations that as a teenager she left God and the church and said, "I'll never come back." That was 20 years ago. Since age 14, she had lived a life of captivity, a life away from God. "I've broken all ten commandments," she said. "You mean God will still accept me?" "Yes," her Christian friend replied, "that's how it is with God." Rosie came home to God in the context of the message: "Jesus Christ came to earth to save you from your sins." The captive was released.

David was a captive in every sense of the word. He was arrested for stealing. He was hooked on drugs. "For a period of seven years I attended a Christian church with my girlfriend, but it never took," he said. He was in jail when I visited him. He was a captive, literally behind bars. "It's like I'm possessed by a demon," he said. "I want to believe, but I just seem unable to have enough faith." I replied, "God forgives us in Christ, David. God sets us free." David is considering coming home. He hasn't quite stepped across the line and committed himself to Christ because he feels unworthy, but I'm confident he will.

Borderline believers, you can come home to God. Unbelievers, aren't you homesick for the One who created you? Prisoners, won't you return to God?

John was on board a ship in a vicious storm in 1736. He turned to some Moravians who were calm in the storm. "Aren't you afraid?" he asked. "No," they replied, "we trust completely in the Lord." John was deeply impressed. Shortly thereafter in a small group Bible study, John heard the introduction to the book of Romans written by Martin Luther and his heart was "strangely warmed." John launched his mission of starting Bible classes throughout England. He rode across England on horseback setting up Bible and prayer groups throughout the land. By the time of his death, he had covered 250,000 miles on horseback for Jesus Christ. John Wesley and his brother Charles also wrote 6,000 Christian hymns including "Love Divine, All Loves Excelling":

Love divine, all loves excelling
Joy of heaven, to earth come down!
Fix in us thy humble dwelling,
All thy faithful mercies crown.

When Christ enters humbled hearts, unworthy people are crowned like royalty.

Jesus thou are all compassion
Pure unbounded love thou art;
Visit with us thy salvation,
Enter every trembling heart.

When Christ enters the trembling heart of the believer, the believer comes home to God. It happens every Christmas.

Finish then thy new creation,
Pure and spotless let us be;
Let us see thy great salvation
Perfectly restored in thee!

When Christ enters hearts filled with sin, righteousness and purity replace self-centeredness. Captives to sin are set free.

Another John, the one for whom Wesley was named, described the good news over 1,700 years before John Wesley got it in terms of restoring God's creation through the redeeming Word.

John Translated The Good News

John, the apostle, says that we can come home to God, because the God who created us "became flesh and dwelt among us full of grace and truth."

In the beginning was the Word, and the Word was with God, and the Word was God. He was in the beginning with God; all things were made through him, and without him was not anything made that was made. In him was life, and the life was the light of men. The light shines in the darkness, and the darkness has not overcome it. There was a man sent from God whose name was John. He came for testimony, to bear witness to the light, that all might believe through him. He was not the light, but came to bear witness to the light.

The true light that enlightens every man was coming into the world. He was in the world, and the world was made through him, yet the world knew him not. He came to his own home, and his own people received him not. But to all who received him, who believed in his name, he gave power to become children of God; who were born, not of blood nor of the will of the flesh nor of the will of man, but of God.

And the Word became flesh and dwelt among us, full of grace and truth; we have beheld his glory, glory as of the only Son from the Father.
— John 1:1-14, RSV

That Jesus dwelt among us, makes it possible for us to come home to God. John translated the good news of Christ in such a way that many captives can come home to God.

Ron, an alcoholic who recently had a heart attack told me, "Old Everett Dirkson from Illinois used to say, 'When the heat goes up, the light goes on.' That's how it is with me. I've been away from God and the church for many years. It took a lot of heat for me to see the light." Ron came home to God. He said, "I used to be a Christmas and Easter Christian." He'd sneak in and sneak out of church twice a year, refusing to sign a visitors' card for fear that someone would follow up on him. "That's all behind me now," he said, "I've come home to where I belong." Ron came home for Christmas. So did Nicolas.

Named after a famous saint, Nicolas had a child-like faith until one day at the orphanage where he had been placed because his father was at war, and his mother could not afford to feed him. Nicolas heard the name of his father in the prayers for English soldiers who had died in World War II. "Right there and then," he said, "I told God I would never believe in him again." We met Nicolas in Lewes, England, when we were there in 1984. He and his wife Jean ran a bed and breakfast where we stayed. We became fast friends. Jean was a new Christian. She was aglow with her new-found faith in Christ. She witnessed to Nicolas, but apparently to no avail. We shared our faith with him as well, but his heart was burdened. He wanted no part of God.

When we returned to England on sabbatical leave in the summer of 1988, we went to Lewes and stayed with Jean and

and Nicolas again. As Jean greeted us, she burst forth with the good news, "Nicolas has become a Christian. It happened last week." We all rejoiced. Two weeks later we heard some bad news. Jean had a lump on her breast. It was cancer. She faced the surgery with great Christian courage, but we wondered what this bad news would do to Nicolas. Would this major tragedy destroy Nicolas' fledgling faith? A quiet man, Nicolas tried hard to express his feelings of fears that now he might lose his wife. Jean continued to witness that Christ would get them through this crisis. Nicolas prayed out loud for the first time at a quiet supper we shared in an English cottage that was more than 400 years old. The prayer was a thing of beauty and simplicity. "God, take care of Jean. And help us to accept whatever happens. Thank you, Jesus, for coming with your comfort. Amen."

The day we left England we heard the good news. The surgery was a success. Our prayers for healing had been answered. Nicolas said, "Praise the Lord." Nicolas had come home to God like the Jewish captives who returned to Jerusalem. Nicolas returned to the light from the darkness of resentment.

John describes the journey from captivity this way:

> *The true light which enlightens every man was coming into the world. He was in the world, and the world was made through him, yet the world knew him not.... But to all who received him, who believed in his name, he gave power to become children of God, who were born, not of blood nor of the will of the flesh, nor of the will of man, but of God.* — John 1:9-13, RSV

Isaiah foretold it. Paul and John translated it. Messengers have picked it up and promulgated the message of good news into every language and situation. "Break into shouts of joy you ruins of Jerusalem! The Lord will rescue his city and comfort his people. The Lord will use his holy power; he will save his people, and all the world will see it (Isaiah 52:9-10, TEV)."

Rosie, David, John, Ron and Nicolas heard the good news and came home to God. So can you.

Christmas 1
1 Samuel 2:18-20, 26

A Mother's Pride And Joy

The story of Samuel is a drama of great intensity, great love, great change, great conflict and great challenge. This story begins with Hannah, in the 11th century B.C., praying to the Lord for a son. She was barren. In ancient times barrenness was a disgrace for a woman.

A Mother's Pride And Joy

As Hanna and her husband arrived at Shiloh for a religious pilgrimage to the place of worship, Hannah prayed. We pick up this prayer at verse one of chapter one of the book of 1 Samuel.

She (Hannah) was in deep anguish and was crying bitterly as she prayed to the Lord. She made this vow: "O Lord of heaven, if you will look down upon my sorrow and answer my prayer and give me a son, then I will give him back to you, and he'll be yours for his entire lifetime . . . (1 Samuel 1:10-11, LB)."

Hannah promised that if God would give her a son, she would dedicate him to the Lord's ministry. Shortly thereafter a son was conceived and born, his mother's pride and joy, a direct answer to prayer. Hannah now had a dilemma. Should she keep her son, and thus preserve the great pride and joy of her life, or keep her vow to give the child for God's ministry as she had promised? She decided to keep her vow. Hannah's real pride and joy was God.

It isn't easy to give up what seems like the most important thing in your life. Who knows the struggle Hannah went through, except perhaps another mother? Hannah loved God more than her own son. After Samuel was weaned at about age three, Hannah took him to the shrine at Shiloh and left him with the priests to raise. She saw him just once a year when she and her husband made a religious pilgrimage to Shiloh. That's dedication! That's sacrifice! The Lord made great use of that mother's dedication. Samuel, the boy priest, "grew in stature and in favor with the Lord and with man (1 Samuel 2:26)," a phrase used about another young man named Jesus at a later time. This "favor with the Lord" included a special revelation.

As a boy Samuel heard his name spoken by God. He thought it was Eli, the priest, calling. The third time Samuel answered "Speak, Lord, for thy servant hears (1 Samuel 3:9)." The Lord told Samuel that Eli and household would suffer because Eli's two sons were corrupt priests. Eli insisted on hearing what the Lord told Samuel. This was the turning point in the boy's life. The boy learned to serve the Lord rather than humankind. Samuel told Eli what the Lord had said about his sons.

Eli's sons were corrupt and selfish priests. They carried the Ark of the Covenant (the box in which the Ten Commandments were kept) into battle with the Philistines. The Ark was captured. Eli fell over dead when he heard what happened. Samuel, the young man, emerged as God's leader of Israel at a time of great need.

Samuel summoned the people to gather at Mizpah, a hilltop north of Jerusalem. He attributed the misfortunes of the people to backsliding and idolatry. He urged the people to fast and pray with repentance. In the next battle with the Philistines, the Lord assisted the Israelites and victory was theirs. A stone was erected to commemorate the victory on a place called Ebenezer ("the Stone of Help"). Samuel became the greatest of the judges of Israel.

As a man, Samuel was the last of the judges. The judges ruled the tribes of Israel through strong personality, moral stature and the belief that they could discern the will of God. The judges rallied the primitive tribes of Israel and helped them emerge as one people. Samuel's dedication inspired the people.

As an old man, Samuel saw his own sons, Joel and Abijah, who were judges in Beersheba, become corrupt, taking bribes and perverting justice, just like the sons of Eli. As in the case of Eli we are reminded that God has no grandchildren. Each generation must rise and make its own commitment. A father's faith does not necessarily rub off on his children. The elders of Israel demanded that Samuel, now too old to rule well, appoint and anoint a king. Reluctantly, Samuel chose Saul (1 Samuel 10:24), fearing that the people would depend too much on their earthly ruler and not enough on their divine ruler.

In the last years of his life Samuel, the prophet-judge, had great conflict with Saul, the new king of Israel. The conflict between Samuel and Saul was based on Saul following his own will instead of the will of God. Samuel anointed a new king, a boy named David, in the town of Bethlehem. The conflict between Saul and David grew. Further complications included David's friendship with Saul's son Jonathan, causing further conflict between Saul and Jonathan.

Samuel's story is an interesting, vibrant story of a mother's pride and joy who emerges as a strong leader of God's people. But what does all this have to do with us? One might shrug his shoulders and say, "So what?" This story is an Old Testament gem, not only because it is an interesting story about a dedicated mother and her dedicated son, but because this story intersects with our lives today.

Two Connections

The first connection with our lives is prayer. We note from the beginning that Hannah did not want a son for her personal reasons. She wanted a son to dedicate to God's service. She was aware of the needs of the people of God as well as her own needs. She prayed within the will of God. In the words of John's Gospel, she prayed "abiding in the Lord like a branch abides in a grape vine."

> *Whatever you ask in my name, I will do it, that the Father may be glorified in the Son; if you ask anything in my name, I will do it.* — John 14:13-14, RSV

Again Jesus said:

> *Abide in me and I in you. As the branch cannot bear fruit by itself, unless it abides in the vine, neither can you, unless you abide in me.* — John 15:4, RSV

The efficacy of prayer, getting results in prayer, goes up in direct proportion to "abiding in God." Hannah's prayer is a model prayer. She sought God, and she sought a son. Because she sought God in prayer, she abided in God. Hannah became a great teacher of the nature of prayer.

Samuel was a great prophet and judge in direct proportion to his abiding in God in prayer. He is considered second only to Moses in abiding in God against great odds and in spite of much criticism and conflict. The conflict he had with King Saul is over this very point. Saul violated the sacred principle of the divine monarchy, following the will of God instead of one's own will. Saul's disobedience of God caused him to follow his own mind and will. Samuel reminds us of the biblical corrective to seek to know and do the will of God. Samuel's sincere attempt to hear God in prayer and follow God in life are examples of integrity, even today.

God used a woman and a boy who knew how to pray to accomplish his purposes. Today women and children have many rights. In ancient Israel they had very few rights. Women and children were generally considered property, not persons.

A Jewish man could divorce his wife for any reason at all by going down to the neighborhood well, saying, "I divorce you," three times as he walked around the well. Thus he would be rid of his wife. Jesus' strong statements against divorce were aimed at this unfair treatment of women.

In the story of Hannah and Samuel we discover that Hannah is an important woman. Hannah is called by God and used by God for his purposes. The story of Hannah is no sentimental tale of a mom who loved her son. The story of Hannah is a story of a woman who loved God more than her son and prayed to God by abiding in God's will. Thus this story is of a mother who teaches us how to pray. God first, then family. Are we open to God speaking through dedicated, devout women today? Are we open to God using children to speak to us?

In ancient Israel children were generally regarded as property, not people. As the boy Samuel emerged as a priest, prophet and judge, the message is clear. Children who abide in God are teachers of God's way. God can use children to bring his message to a friend, a neighborhood or a nation.

The boy Samuel said, "Speak Lord, for thy servant hears." The boy Samuel is used by God to correct the adult, Eli. The student taught the teacher! Are we open to God speaking through children today? Jesus' treatment of children is remarkable. "Let the children come unto me and forbid them not, for of such is the kingdom of God," Jesus says.

The second connection between the story of Samuel and our lives is summarized in the word "priorities." In dedicating and re-dedicating themselves to God, Hannah and Samuel are good examples to us. Hannah preached the nature of priorities by her lifestyle. So did Samuel. In calling the nation to repentance and prayer, young Samuel is calling us as well. Don't we need renewal today? Don't God's people fall into the trap of putting other things before God? Don't we need repentance and a deeper prayer life today? How much sacrifice are we willing to make for God and God's mission?

The story of Samuel is a story of the renewing of God's people. The church of today needs renewal. That's the point of Pentecost, the festival of celebrating the beginnings of the Christian church. The call goes out across the land. The Holy Spirit creates faith in our hearts and brings us together as a church to fulfill God's mission to bring all people to faith in him. Those in high and mighty positions can do it; so can obscure and seemingly unimportant people. God can call and use anyone today. "Speak, Lord, for thy servant hears."

Christmas 2
Jeremiah 31:6-14

Mourning Turned To Joy

The 14th canticle from the Lutheran Book of Worship poetically summarizes Jeremiah 31:6-14:

Listen! you nations of the world:
 listen to the Word of the Lord.
Announce it from coast to coast;
 declare it to distant islands.

The Lord who scattered Israel will
 gather his people again;
and he will keep watch over them as a
 shepherd watches his flock.

With shouts of joy they will come,
 their faces radiantly happy,
for the Lord is so gen'rous to them;
 He showers his people with gifts.

Young women will dance for joy,
 and men young and old will make merry.
Like a garden refreshed by the rain,
 they will never be in want again.

Break into shouts of great joy:
 Jacob is free again!
Teach nations to sing the song:
 "The Lord has saved his people!"

The historical context of this Scriptural emphasis on "shouts of great joy" replacing mourning is the predicted return of the people of God from the Babylonian captivity. The Hebrews had been taken as slaves in 587 B.C. There in Babylon the people lived in bondage and hopelessness for many years. There they hung up their harps on willow trees for they could sing no more. There misery moved in like a fog. There weeping and wailing could be heard everywhere. In Jeremiah 31, a prediction was spoken that meant the darkness would be turned into light; mourning into joy.

Slavery to foreigners would cease; the yoke of bondage to the Babylonians would be broken; freedom would be experienced. "They (the people of God) will come back from the land of the enemy. There is hope for your future, says the Lord (Jeremiah 31:16-17)." A new covenant with the law written on stone tablets (Jeremiah 31:31-34).

This predicted time of hope, joy and fulfillment was experienced by the people of God in about 517 B.C. as they returned to Jerusalem from Babylonian captivity and rebuilt the temple. In this historical movement back home we have a parable of the movement from sad to glad in our lives.

Why So Sad?

Why were the Israelites so sad? How are we like them in this sadness? Some of the mourning in Babylon came because of sin and the refusal to acknowledge that sin against God and other people. The major sin was idolatry.

> *. . . They have burned incense to other gods and worshiped the works of their own hand (Jeremiah 1:16).*
>
> *Your wickedness will chasten you, and your apostasy will reprove you. Know and see that it is evil and bitter for you to forsake the Lord your God . . ." (Jeremiah 2:19).*
>
> *Their idols are like scarecrows in a cucumber field, and they cannot speak; they have to be carried, for they cannot walk (Jeremiah 10:5).*
>
> *. . . Have you seen what she did, that faithless one, Israel, how she went up on every high hill and under every green tree, and there played the harlot? And I thought, "After she has done all this she will return to me"; but she did not return . . . (Jeremiah 3:6-7).*

Idolatry is like adultery. It is faithlessness! Often we become dull to God in such circumstances. The lack of repentance characterized the people of God in Jeremiah's day.

> ". . . Behold I will bring you to judgment for saying, 'I have not sinned' (Jeremiah 2:35)."

Part of Israel's sadness came from facing the consequences of giving one's highest loyalty to something or someone other than the one true God. The ultimate, often repeated, sin of Israel was idolatry, chasing after man-made gods. Sound familiar? The refusal to acknowledge sin compounded their problems. Sound familiar? Ethical relativism in our day results in rationalization instead of repentance. This Word of God in Jeremiah is the biblical corrective for people of every generation who excuse their behavior instead of repenting before God for what they have done.

From brassy materialism to the new fad called the New Age Movement, idolatry has crept in like a fog and captured people today as of old. Idolatry has brought with it a sadness which psychologists today call *anomie* — the inability to feel one's own feelings. "The Living Dead" is the name of a rock group. "The living dead" is also a description of the "Me Generation," rationalizing away its sins until the state of sadness and mourning take over and inhibit expression of feelings. Part of Israel's sadness was facing the consequences of idolatry.

Another part of the Israelites' mourning was the separation from their home land. Separation from one's home and family brings deep sadness. The people of God were lonely in Babylon. Loneliness was like a communicable disease in Babylon. In our time too, loneliness permeates people's lives. Mother Theresa of Calcutta, India, while visiting America said that the biggest problem in the world is not physical hunger but loneliness. She said, "I see it everywhere here in America."

Many people today are like detached leaves, falling from the source of life, into a pile of other detached leaves, beginning the process of shriveling up for death. What is needed is a transplantation back into the tree of life. We need to be saved.

Israel needed nothing less than salvation. We need that salvation, too. In the Bible, salvation does not just mean going to heaven when we die. Only one-fifth of the 150 references to "save" or "saved" in the New Testament refer to the consummation at the last day, according to Alan Richardson's *Theological Word Study of the Bible*. Nearly one-third of the New Testament references denote deliverance from specific ills such as captivity, disease and devil possession.

Like Israel, we need to be saved from a wide variety of ills, including many which we have brought upon ourselves. We are not far from the truth when we characterize our time in terms of spiritual captivity, the disease of loneliness and demonic separation from self, other people and God. We are languishing. Thus the promise of Jeremiah 31 is a welcome word of salvation: ". . . They shall languish no more (Jeremiah 31:12)." ". . . The Lord has saved his people, the remnant of Israel (Jeremiah 31:7)." ". . . I will turn their mourning into joy, I will comfort them, and give them gladness for sorrow (Jeremiah 31:13)."

Gladness Instead Of Sadness

Listen, you nations of the world. Israel's return to Jerusalem was marked by the redeeming work of God: "For the Lord has ransomed Jacob (another name for Israel) and has redeemed him from hands too strong for him (Jeremiah 31:11)." The return to Jerusalem is a product of God's forgiving redemption and restoration of his people based on the recognition that the enemies we fight are too strong for us.

Listen, you nations of the world. How do we appropriate this redemption? How are we ransomed from our languishing? How do we defeat enemies "whose hands are too strong for us"? Just like Israel — through repentance and faith. Turning away from false gods which save no one; turning back to the God of our salvation is the biblical corrective for lostness and languishing in every age.

Jeremiah describes the turn back to God like this:

Let not the wise man glory in his wisdom,
let not the mighty man glory in his might,
let not the rich man glory in his riches,
but let him who glories glory in this,
that he understands and knows me,
that I am the Lord who practices kindness,
justice and righteousness in the earth;
for in these things I delight, says the Lord.
— Jeremiah 9:23-24

Listen, you nations of the world. Gladness comes from restoration. Israel returned home. The invitation to come home to God is offered to all people everywhere.

Listen, you nations of the world. Isaiah, the prophet, describes this homecoming to God in terms of depending on God rather than self. He calls this depending on God "waiting for the Lord." This turning back to God means that we can "fly" to heavenly perspectives.

Have you not known? Have you not heard? The Lord is the everlasting God, the Creator of the ends of the earth. He does not faint or grow weary, his understanding is unsearchable. He gives power to the faint, and to him who has no might he increases strength. Even youths shall faint and be weary, the young men shall fall exhausted; but they who wait for the Lord shall renew their strength, they shall mount up with wings like eagles, they shall run and not be weary, they shall walk and not faint." — Isaiah 40:28-31

Listen, you nations of the world. According to Isaiah, the trip back home shall include flying and running and walking. This trip shall also include singing (Jeremiah 31:12) and dancing (Jeremiah 31:13) and feasting (Jeremiah 31:14).

Listen! you nations of the world:
listen to the Word of the Lord.
Announce it from coast to coast;
declare it to distant islands.

*The Lord who scattered Israel will
    gather his people again;
And he will keep watch over them as a
    shepherd watches his flock.*

*With shouts of joy they will come,
    their faces radiantly happy,
for the Lord is so gen'rous to them;
    He showers his people with gifts.*

*Young women will dance for joy,
    and men young and old will make merry.
Like a garden refreshed by the rain,
    they will never be in want again.*

*Break into shouts of great joy:
    Jacob is free again!
Teach nations to sing the song:
    "The Lord has saved his people!"*

Listen, you nations of the world. Listen to the Word of the Lord.

The Baptism Of Our Lord
Isaiah 61:1-4

Anointed

Isaiah 61 is a dangerous text! Jesus used this text to launch his ministry in his home town of Nazareth and it caused him to be thrown out of the synagogue and taken to the edge of a cliff. Jesus' life was threatened as a result of his reading, interpretation and application of this text. "Today, this Scripture is being fulfilled in your hearing," Jesus said. But we are getting ahead of our story. Let's go back to the original context of Isaiah 61 before we return to Jesus' use of the text.

Isaiah's Anointed Ministry

This portion of Scripture was apparently written in the context of the Babylonian captivity of the Jewish people from 587 to about 517 B.C. The liberation of the afflicted captives and the freedom of the prisoners mentioned in verse one apparently refers to the return of the Jews from Babylon to Jerusalem after 70 years of exile in Babylon. This text has to do with restoration and renewal through healing ministries of binding the brokenhearted and comforting the afflicted by God's anointed prophet. God's anointed servant calls the people to be healed and receive favor from Yahweh. To be anointed means to be called and chosen by God.

"The year of the Lord's favor" may have two meanings. First of all, it is a clear reference to the fact that the time of punishment for sins has passed, that through repentance, the people have now come back into favor with God who has punished them for their disobedience. The second meaning is drawn from Leviticus 25. The second meaning is that the "year of favor" is the jubilee.

> *You shall . . . consecrate the fiftieth year and proclaim a release through the land to all its inhabitants. It shall be a jubilee for you, and each of you shall return to his own property, and each of you shall return to his family.*
>
> *You shall have the fiftieth year as a jubilee; you shall not sow, nor reap its aftergrowth, nor gather in from its untrimmed vines.*
>
> *For it is a jubilee, it shall be holy to you. You shall eat its crops out of the field . . . .*
>
> *If you make a sale, moreover, to your friend, or buy from a friend, or buy from your friend's hand, you shall not wrong one another . . . .*
>
> *So you shall not wrong one another, but you shall fear your God; for I am the Lord your God.*
>
> — Leviticus 25:10-17, NAB

The jubilee was a time of restoration and refreshment for the land and for the people. It was a time to recall God's graciousness and for God's people to be gracious. The jubilee was a time of generosity and forgiveness because God is generous and forgiving. For Isaiah 61 to recall the jubilee described in Leviticus while the people were in exile was to remind them of God's gracious generosity and to invite them to minister to one another with the same spirit. This type of gracious generosity is also the theme of Jesus' use of this text at the inaugural address of his ministry in Nazareth.

Jesus' Anointed Ministry

In chapter three of Luke's gospel, we hear about the baptism of Jesus in the Jordan River. This baptism is the anointing of Jesus and the beginning of his ministry. In chapter four of Luke we hear about the 40-day temptation of Jesus by demonic forces. This was his exile or time of aloneness. The desert temptations of Jesus show that the jubilee of Jesus' ministry is preceded by a dark period . . . a valley of shadows to use the imagery of the 23rd Psalm, just as the exiled Jews had experienced forsakenness in the shadowy exile in Babylon.

When we go through the valley of shadows and temptations, we can be assured that Jesus is with us because we know he has been there. When we are tempted, we know that he was tempted, too. He got through. So can we. He got on with ministry. So can we. "He began his teaching in their synagogues and was praised by all (Luke 4:15)," until he came to Nazareth, the town in which he was raised by Mary and Joseph.

In Nazareth the initial reception was positive. "Hometown boy makes good" might have been a headline in the local Nazareth morning newspaper, if they had had newspapers back then. The whole town showed up for sabbath worship at the local synagogue because it was rumored that Jesus who was making a big hit all over Galilee would be there.

Sure enough, Jesus was there. Sure enough, he spoke. The atmosphere was electric with anticipation. You could have heard a pin drop when the ex-carpenter of Nazareth got up to interpret the Word. The intensity of the moment grew dramatically when the young preacher read Isaiah 61:1-2 as the beginning of his inaugural address.

"The spirit of the Lord is upon me," Jesus began, apparently recalling his baptism by John and the Word of the Lord God: ". . . Thou art my beloved Son . . . (Luke 3:22)." The mood of the assembly began to change as Jesus sat down and said with authority: "Today this Scripture has been fulfilled in your hearing." The fact that he sat down meant that he saw himself as the chairperson. The fact that he spoke with authority meant that he saw himself as the author.

In a recent visit to England, I saw the sitting Jesus over the altar in many cathedrals. I asked one of the tour guides about the sitting position. He explained, "In Jewish tradition, the one who sits is in charge. That's where we get our word 'chairperson'."

It's one thing for a hometown boy to come home and the people to celebrate his new-found celebrity status; it's quite another for this young preacher to refuse to go along with sentimental celebration of his status and insist that the people pay attention to and follow the Word.

With authority Jesus said, "Today this Word is fulfilled in your midst." The root of the word "authority" is "right, based on origin." It is the author who has authority. Jesus was claiming "author's rights." The author had entered the story as one of the characters. It's no wonder that we frequently read in the gospels, "Jesus spoke as one with authority."

Now things began to heat up and really get dangerous. Jesus was speaking with authority. He actually expected his friends and neighbors to change, to do something based on the Word, not just to smile and say how proud they were of him. Something clicked behind his eyes. The people sensed it. The tense atmosphere got more tense as Jesus read what was in the hearts of his former neighbors, rejection of the Word. He reminded them that both Elijah and Elisha were rejected by the multitudes and were able to minister only to a few people because the hearts of most were hard against the Word (Luke 4:25-27). Jesus added fuel to the fire as he said, "A prophet is not without honor, except in his own town (Luke 4:24)."

Restlessness now turned to anger and hatred. The Word has a way of cutting through illusions. We don't like to have our preconceptions punctured. We don't like to have our apparent acceptance called rejection and our apparent cheers called jeers especially when the person speaking is right on target and speaks with authority.

Thus we move from the synagogue of friends and neighbors to the edge of the cliff where enemies try to rid themselves permanently of this bad-news dispenser who claimed he fulfilled the Isaiah prophecy of good news. His neighbors tried to murder Jesus by throwing him over a cliff. But as they tried to get rid of their problems by murder, suddenly something startling happened which made this strange day even stranger. We pick up the story in verse 29 of chapter 4 of Luke:

> *. . . and they rose up and cast him out of the city, and led him to the brow of the hill on which their city had been built, in order to throw him down the cliff. But passing through their midst, he went on his way.*

Imagine it: mob violence, murder on their minds, rage feeding rage, the blasphemer who was pushed out the door of the synagogue out to the edge of the cliff suddenly turned and looked at the neighbors — turned gang — and then he walked through the midst of them. That's authority. He was truly the anointed one, the author with rights based on origin.

A Jubilee For You And Me?

This is a dangerous text because Jesus made it his own. Favor, comfort, gladness, building, repair — these are Jesus' ways of ministry, a ministry he expects all who follow him to use as a pattern. In other words, all the baptized are anointed and called to minister by: proclaiming good news to the afflicted, freeing people who are captives to a variety of addictions; binding up the brokenhearted by solidarity with them; helping people see reality instead of living in illusions; and celebrating the jubilee of God's generous ministry by ministering generously.

Jubilee means ministry. The baptism of Jesus and the inaugural address which follows it are models for ministry. It is simply not enough to be admirers in the grandstand. God anoints us in baptism and invites us to leave the grandstand and get into the action of real ministry. Will there be a jubilee for you and me? That depends on whether we recognize that we have been anointed in baptism for ministry. Ministry means genuine and generous servanthood (ministry).

Jubilee means generosity. Instead of just getting by, God wants us to give of ourselves generously. "God loves a cheerful (literally 'hilarious') giver" since God himself is generous — always more willing to give and forgive than we are to ask and repent, always giving grace to the sinner who repents, always restoring lost children to full family status.

Is this jubilee for you and me? Of course, but first we've got to see it God's way: the new way, the way of generosity and ministry. Giving our time and talents and treasures for

God's ministry is the challenge of this text. Giving generously is the invitation to jubilee living. Why do most of us have more than we need for food, clothes and housing? That's a good question for each of us to consider. I can think of only one good reason: to give it back to God and people with generosity.

Is the jubilee for you and me? Are we tithing with gladness? Are we giving offerings beyond the biblical tithe? That's a good question in relation to this Word of God.

Is this jubilee for you and me? Are we waiting with hope for the second coming of Christ? "Stay on the alert," Jesus says, "for you do not know which day the Lord is coming . . . (Matthew 24:42)." Staying alert is a way to get set to go for God with generosity.

Is this jubilee for you and for me? That depends on our answer to an even more important question: Is this Scripture being fulfilled in us today?

Epiphany 2
Isaiah 62:1-5

From Inferiority To Fulfillment

A counselor was listening carefully to a teenager. She was speaking about her troubles. She felt out of sorts with everyone and everything. She was depressed. Everything was going wrong. Her recent marriage was on the rocks. There was trouble with the baby who had been born recently. Her job was not working out. After listening to her litany of troubles for a long time, the counselor asked her, "Do you believe that God loves everyone?" "Yes," she said, "I'm a Christian. I believe that God loves everyone." "Do you believe that God loves you?" the counselor asked. After a long pause, she said, "No! I don't believe that God loves me." "Why?" asked the counselor. "Because I am not worthy of God's love," the young woman replied. "That is the heart of your problem," the wise counselor replied. "You don't believe in yourself because you feel unworthy, and you feel unworthy because you feel unloved. The place to start," said the counselor, "is for you to believe that God loves you. Grow into it and go for it with all your heart." "I will," the young woman replied. "I'll try to believe that I am loved. You being a good friend who listens to me will help."

Forsaken

In one respect the young woman is like the Jews in captivity in the sixth century B.C. The prophet Isaiah (the scholars usually call him Second Isaiah) brings the corrective to the discouraged, downhearted people of God in these words:

"Yahweh takes delight in you (Isaiah 62:4, JB)."

The Revised Standard Version puts it this way: "You shall be called *My Delight*." Today's English Version says that

Israel's new name is, "God is Pleased with Her." The Living Bible says, "Your new name will be 'The Land of God's Delight' and 'The bride,' for the Lord delights in you and will claim you as his own." In Hebrew the word is *Hephzi-bah,* which is the ultimate affirmation. Literally this Hebrew word means "My delight is in her."

The affirmation is of great consequence, especially because the Jews in exile in Babylonia had felt utterly forsaken by Yahweh. For 70 years in Babylonian captivity the Jews had felt forsaken. Now, at this point in history, Yahweh's prophet brings stirring words of affirmation:

> *. . . no longer will you be called 'Forsaken,' nor your land 'Abandoned,' but you shall be called 'My Delight,' and your land 'The wedded'; for Yahweh takes delight in you . . .*   — Isaiah 62:4, JB

The feelings of forsakenness had resulted from the sins of the people. They had committed idolatry and had repeatedly broken God's laws about idolatry, adultery, stealing and sabbath breaking. They had been caught in the chaos of materialism and selfishness. They had neglected justice and concern for the needy. Their sins had come crashing in on them as the Babylonians conquered them in 587 B.C. In exile, they felt far from God and far from home. They felt like so many ugly wallflowers about whom no one speaks with kindness. The prophet of Yahweh comes offering a proposal of marriage: "You are my Delight, my Bride," says the Lord.

Most of us at one time or another have felt forsaken. Some people have felt that way most of their lives. Forsakenness is the feeling of being abandoned, deserted, rootless, filled with despair, suffering without hope.

In his book, *A Place for You,* Dr. Paul Tournier tells of a young student who had many difficulties. Anxiety never left him. Anxiety sometimes took the form of panic and flight. "Basically," he said, "I'm always looking for a place — for somewhere to be."

The boy had felt rejection by his parents. Vainly he struggled to reconcile to his parents, but the effort proved hopeless. Anger and antagonism were felt by the boy to such an extent that he felt he had no home. The parents' divorce complicated matters considerably because, like many children of divorced parents, he felt he was responsible for their problem. Unconscious forces kept him in a state of inaction. Painful memories were not resolved. He might be renamed, "Forsaken."

The boy's parents put up a pretense of middle-class respectability. That complicated the problem. The parents seemed to the boy to be demanding and totally lacking in understanding of his point of view. That complicated the problem further. He felt rootless. When his best friend, also a troubled youth, committed suicide, the boy said that life was meaningless. He experienced an incapacity for real attachment. He said he wanted love, but he rejected it whenever it was offered, for fear that he would be dumped. He felt deserted. He felt immobilized. He couldn't go on because he had not felt the affirmation of anyone. He had to grow into the feeling of approval before he could go into the world as a productive citizen. Dr. Tournier tried to convey God's affirmation by finding many ways to show the boy his delight in his being. The counselor tried to give the boy "a place to be."

While most of us do not experience this pain of separation to the extent of this troubled teenager, we intuitively identify with his feeling of a lack of a home and his lack of love. Therefore, like Israel of old and like the boy, we too need to hear the words, "Yahweh takes delight in you (Isaiah 62:4)."

My Delight

There is nothing more important for young people today than the affirmation that they are genuinely loved. Most of the unsocial behavior and many of the crimes of youth come from this feeling of forsakenness. Drugs and alcohol abuse originate for many because of this feeling of forsakenness and rootlessness. How important it is that youth today discover the God who takes delight in them.

The story of Jesus at the wedding feast at Cana is about this God of affirmation, although this may not be clear at first reading.

> *On the third day there was a marriage at Cana in Galilee, and the mother of Jesus was there; Jesus also was invited to the marriage, with his disciples. When the wine gave out, the mother of Jesus said to him, "They have no wine." And Jesus said to her, "O woman, what have you to do with me? My hour has not yet come." His mother said to the servants, "Do whatever he tells you." Now six stone jars were standing there, for the Jewish rites of purification, each holding twenty or thirty gallons. Jesus said to them, "Fill the jars with water." And they filled them up to the brim. He said to them, "Now draw some out, and take it to the steward of the feast." So they took it. When the steward of the feast tasted the water now become wine, and did not know where it came from (though the servants who had drawn the water knew), the steward of the feast called the bridegroom and said to him, "Every man serves the good wine first; and when men have drunk freely, then the poor wine; but you have kept the good wine until now." This, the first of his signs, Jesus did at Cana in Galilee, and manifested his glory; and his disciples believed in him.*
> — John 2:1-11 RSV

The point of this first miracle of Jesus in Cana is that Jesus takes water and makes wine out of it. Water is ordinary. Wine is extra ordinary. This first sign of Jesus' ministry is that wherever he goes, he takes ordinary people and makes them extraordinary, extraordinary. Jesus brings this ultimate affirmation to people by "taking delight in us."

In his book, *Extraordinary Living for Ordinary Men,* Sam Shoemaker, one of the co-founders of Alcoholics Anonymous, makes the point that the wedding at Cana means that Jesus came to give us new life and that everywhere we let him in,

Jesus continues to do extraordinary things with ordinary people like us. You alone will get nowhere, but you and Jesus Christ together make an unconquerable partnership for extraordinary living. It all depends on whether or not we believe this Word: "Yahweh delights in you."

Before you ever turn to God, "Yahweh delights in you." Before you ever repent of your sins, "Yahweh delights in you." Before you believe in God, God believes in you, "Yahweh delights in you." While you are yet a sinner, Christ died for you. His cross is the extra, the plus that proves once and for all, "Yahweh delights in you."

Each Sunday as we worship, we hear these blessed words, "Yahweh delights in you," in one form or another. The 3,200-year-old benediction is used every Sunday at the end of the service:

The Lord bless you and keep you
The Lord make his face shine upon you
and be gracious to you
The Lord look upon you with favor and give you peace.

That's our weekly reminder that God is smiling at us. Think of it: Yahweh, who created the heavens and the earth, before whom all nations and rulers will one day bow, smiles at you. "Yahweh delights in you!"

Epiphany 3
Nehemiah 8:1-4a, 5-6, 8-10
The Water Gate And The Word Proclaimed

The story of Nehemiah and Ezra is a drama in three parts. The first part takes place in the sixth century B.C. in Babylon where the Persians under King Cyrus conquered the Babylonians and decreed that the exiled Israelites could return home to Jerusalem.

Nehemiah, a Jew living in Babylon at peace with the Persians, rose to a place of honor as a royal cup-bearer in the Persian court. In about 445 B.C., Nehemiah received a message from a relative who had just returned from a visit in Jerusalem. The relative, Hanani, reported bad news:

> *The survivors there in the province who escaped exile are in great trouble and shame; the wall of Jerusalem is broken down, and its gates are destroyed by fire.*
> — Nehemiah 1:3

Deeply moved by the report and remembering the promises to Moses that God would redeem the Children of Israel, Nehemiah determined to return to Jerusalem and help rebuild the destroyed city. He got permission from the Persian ruler to return to his homeland.

Part two of the drama has Nehemiah returning to the land of his fathers and undertaking the task of rebuilding the city of Jerusalem. This man of God called the Jewish leaders together and proposed the refortification of the holy city. They responded eagerly: "Let us rise up and build (Nehemiah 2:18)." Each of the business merchants and priests worked hard to rebuild a section of the fortification of Jerusalem, opposite his home. This is the context for the entrance of Ezra, the scholar-preacher who took the building theme beyond buildings. Ezra proclaimed the Word of God to rebuild the people.

Part three of this drama is today and what the Word of God in this story means to us. But I'm getting ahead of my story. First let us look at Ezra's sermon on rebuilding people.

Proclaiming The Word At The Water Gate

Ezra had led an expedition of the Jews back to Jerusalem from Babylon. Rumor had it that this priest of the Most High God had in his possession a copy of the Scriptures. The day came when a large wooden pulpit was erected near the Water Gate in Jerusalem and Ezra dramatically mounted this pulpit and read from the Scriptures (probably the first five books of what we Christians call the Old Testament). We pick up the story from Nehemiah's account in the *Living Bible:*

> *Now in mid-September, all the people assembled at the plaza in front of the Water Gate and requested Ezra, their religious leader, to read to them the law of God which he had given to Moses. So Ezra the priest brought out to them the scroll of Moses' laws . . . He faced the square in front of the Water Gate, and read from early morning until noon. Everyone stood up as he opened the scroll . . . All the people began sobbing when they heard the commands of the law.* — Nehemiah 8:1-9, LB

Why did the thousands of people in Jerusalem cry when they heard the law of Moses? Because it had been a long time since they had heard it read? Yes, but the deep emotion of the moment also had to do with the realization that they had drifted far from the ways of God. They wept for their sins. What an interesting association we have here between the Jewish repentance at the Water Gate and the American shame connected with the hotel of the same name in Jerusalem.

At the Water Gate, from the high pulpit, the preacher reached deep within his soul and called the people to a higher understanding of God. He said:

> *. . . Do not cry on such a day as this! For today is a sacred day before the Lord your God — it is a time*

to celebrate with a hearty meal, and to send presents to those in need, for the joy of the Lord is your strength. You must not be dejected and sad!
— Nehemiah 8:9-10, LB

This dramatic story ends on the high note of joy, a wonderful serendipity whenever the Word of God is preached. People expect somber and sad consequences when the Word of God is proclaimed. Instead, often exalted joy comes.

In our day, the Scripture has been long neglected by God's people. Many Christians are nearly illiterate when it comes to the Scriptures. One of the biblical correctives we hear in this story is to get back to the Bible.

The story is told of the pastor who visited a Sunday school class one day. "Question my students all you like," said the teacher. "Who broke down the walls of Jericho?" the pastor asked. Johnny quickly responded, "Not me. I didn't do it, pastor." The pastor with a pained look said to the teacher, "Is this kind of response typical in this class?" The teacher said defensively, "Pastor, I know Johnny. If he said he didn't do it, he didn't do it."

The dazed pastor sought out the Sunday school superintendent and told him the story. He replied: "That is our best class. I'm sure no one in the class is guilty." A few days later the pastor reported the incident to the official board. The treasurer quickly spoke up: "Pastor, I move that we pay for the damage and charge it to upkeep." There certainly is a great need to improve our biblical knowledge!

In many church newsletters Bible readings are listed encouraging members to read the Bible each day. Daily reading from the Bible brings unexpected joys to those who do it. Joys come from biblical knowledge. God's ways may initially cause us sadness because we realize our sins, but joy comes because God wants to give us his kingdom. Reading the Scriptures can bring us closer to God and bring us unexpected joys.

One dear old Christian lady was asked, "Why are you so happy all the time?" "I read the Bible for two hours a day," she replied. "Why do you do that?" her friends asked. She replied with a smile, "Just cramming for the final exams!"

It isn't just the final exams at the end of life, but life itself which is enriched by the reading of God's Word. Ezra proclaimed the Word. He also called the people to follow the Word.

Following The Word

The great Christian scholar, Karl Barth, says that there are three ways in which the Word of God comes to us today. First and foremost the Word of God is Jesus Christ. The Gospel of John says, "In the beginning was the Word and the Word was with God, and the Word was God . . . and the Word became flesh and dwelt among us full of grace and truth (John 1:1-14, RSV).''

In other words, when Christ is proclaimed and believed, when he is embraced by faith, people find the exalted joy they were intended to know when they were born. "I came to give life in abundance," Jesus said.

The second form of the Word is the written Word, the Bible. The Bible is God's Word because it is the primary means by which we know Christ and God's ways. The Bible provides light for the spiritual pilgrim and strength for the journey. The Bible provides correctives for our wrong ideas about God, about ourselves and about life. The Bible helps us see illusions for what they are — false ideas. The Bible grounds us in the reality of God.

The third form of the Word today is preaching or proclaiming. That brings us full circle back to Ezra and our text. Not only did Ezra and his helpers read the Scripture to the people at the Water Gate; they interpreted the Word to the people. They preached the Word. That interpretation brought the sadness of realization that the people had been living illusions because they had been far away from God, but the gladness that God still loved them and accepted them which brought exalted joy. The people embraced the Word.

The exposition and interpretation of God's Word brings life. Paul writes in Romans 10:13-17:

> ... *Everyone who calls on the name of the Lord will be saved. But how are men to call upon him in whom they have not believed? And how are they to believe in him of whom they have never heard? And how are they to hear without a preacher? And how can men preach unless they are sent? . . . So faith comes from what is heard, and what is heard comes by the preaching of Christ.*

Preaching Christ is expository preaching. Luther observed that the Old Testament is the cradle of Christ. Interpreting all Scripture in the light of Christ's coming helps us to apply Scripture to our lives. This is what Luther meant by *"solo Scriptura."*

Application as well as interpretation is necessary for preaching to result in changed lives. To have proclaimed the Word fully, the hearers must make the connection with their own lives. In Jerusalem at the Water Gate on that dramatic day when Ezra preached, the people soaked up the Word and applied the Word. That meant sadness for shortcomings and gladness for the grace of God. That experience of law and gospel has been experienced by millions upon millions of people since Ezra's day.

Another important aspect of preaching is illustration. Preaching is more than interpretation of what a text says. Preaching is even more than immediate application to our lives. Illustrations can bring the interpretation of the Word to life, and provides inroads to the subconscious mind which produces fruits of righteousness at later times. Stories and anecdotes help the people to grasp and embrace the Word as their own. In crisis situations, stories can be called forth to help with difficult decisions.

Many come to church expecting stern rebuke for their fallenness, only to discover the incomparable joy of acceptance, love and Christian fellowship as they gather under the Word of God. Under the Word, many have found faith in Christ as a way of life, the Bible as a guide for our pathways in life, and the preaching of God's Word as the reminder of God and his ways for the living of life to its fullest with the greatest possible joy.

Thanks Ezra, we needed that!

Epiphany 4
Jeremiah 1:4-10

Dispelling Ministry Illusions

Jeremiah is often regarded as a Christ-figure, a prophet like Jesus, who suffered at the hands of his own people because he loved them enough to tell them the truth. A God-inspired man, fearlessly denouncing the religious laxity and social ills of his day, Jeremiah paid the price for his words. Tradition says that in 587 B.C., when the Babylonians conquered Jerusalem as Jeremiah had predicted, his own people murdered him.

The text we have before us is the call to ministry of the prophet Jeremiah in about 627 B.C., the 13th year of King Josiah's reign. From the beginning we notice that Jeremiah 1:4-10 dispels ministry illusions.

Illusions are false ideas. There are at least three false ideas about ministry which are dispelled in this Word of God about the call: that ministry is for priests alone; that feelings of inferiority will keep us from serving; and that fears will keep us from ministering.

The biblical correctives for these illusions are: that the ministry is for all the people of God; that the power and gifts of God turn inferior-feeling people into effective leaders; and that the affirmation "I will be with you" makes all the difference in the world.

The Priesthood Of The People

Jeremiah was the son of a priest. He was born in the town of Anathoth, a village three miles northeast of Jerusalem which was set aside for the priestly tribe of the Levites in the time of Joshua. In Jeremiah's time there were many priests who made this town their home. Jeremiah grew up around priests, but as far as we know, never "took holy orders" or became a priest. As a called layman, Jeremiah, the prophet, severely criticized the priesthood and ritualistic religion which gave false security.

As a matter of fact, Jeremiah stood before the temple and roared these words to the spiritually hard-of-hearing:

> *Be appalled, O heavens, at this, be shocked, be utterly desolate, says the Lord, for my people have committed two evils: they have forsaken me, the fountain of living waters, and hewed out cisterns for themselves, broken cisterns, that can hold no water.*
> — Jeremiah 2:12-13, RSV

The people of God went through the rituals of religion, but in their hearts, the temples within, they worshiped false gods. They were faithless!

> *Surely, as a faithless wife leaves her husband, so have you been faithless to me, O house of Israel, says the Lord.*
> — Jeremiah 3:20, RSV

The threat of punishment looms large in this prophet of God who is called to "uproot and pull down, to destroy and to overthrow . . . (Jeremiah 1:10 TEV)."

> *An appalling and horrible thing has happened in the land: the prophets prophesy falsely, and the priests rule at their direction; my people love to have it so, but what will you do when the end comes?*
> — Jeremiah 5:30-31, RSV

Jeremiah opposed the temple religion and priestly pomp and circumstance which lacked moral fiber and ethical behavior.

> *. . . From prophet to priest every one deals falsely. They have healed the wound of my people lightly, saying "Peace, peace, when there is no peace."*
> — Jeremiah 8:10-11, RSV

In other words, Jeremiah attacked religion which had no heart for God and advocated the Word of God as a club to destroy priestly religion which brought comfort without truth.

Martin Luther did the same thing in the 16th century. One of the great principles of Luther is "the priesthood of the baptized." Luther taught that all of God's people, not just the priests, have responsibility to minister. The word minister means servant. The one who truly serves God and people is the true minister; not just those with turned around collars! The word "layperson" which we often use to denote a non-professional, comes from the Bible word *"laos"* which means "the people" (the people of God). A layman is one who serves God. That's no second-class citizenship! Illusion number one: "We are not ordained clergy." Down. Two to go!

The Power Of God Is Discovered In The Gifts Of The People

"I don't know how to speak; I am too young . . .," Jeremiah initially protested. Similar feelings are experienced today before the sweeping claims of God who expects his baptized people to act for him: "I'm not eloquent." "I'm too young." "I'm too old." "I'm not capable." "I'm too weak." "I can't do it."

At baptism God gives us the gift of the Holy Spirit. In life as God calls us to serve him and people, he supplies gifts for the Spirit for the work of the people of God. We can discover the will of God in our lives by discovering our spiritual gifts. Spiritual gifts are God's signature on our souls.

God says, "Do not say, 'I am too young, but go to the people . . .' (Jeremiah 1:7, TEV)." In other words, Jeremiah was gifted to go for God. In the same manner, God gives gifts to all his people.

Paul puts it this way:

> *Now concerning spiritual gifts, brethren, I do not want you to be uninformed . . . . There are varieties of*

gifts, but the same Spirit, and there are varieties of service, but the same Lord; and there are varieties of working, but it is the same God who inspires them all in every one. To each is given the manifestation of the Spirit for the common good . . . Now you are the body of Christ and individually members of it.
— 1 Corinthians 12:1-27, RSV

Illusion number two, "We can't do it." Down; one to go.

Fear Isn't In Charge Here

"Do not be afraid of them, for I will be with you to protect you (Jeremiah 1:8, TEV)." Fear is one of the most serious inhibiting factors for all people, including the people of God. In a recent Bible study, I asked the group to name the fears they feel themselves and/or observe in others. Here is the list which emerged in three groupings. (1) Illnesses: sickness, growing old, and dying; (2) Physical/psychological dangers: wars (especially nuclear war), terrorists, traffic in large cities, and the unknown, and; (3) Family: especially for children and grandchildren in a drug-oriented culture.

That's quite a bushelful, isn't it? That's enough to inhibit ministry until the kingdom comes. That's why God intends to quiet our fears.

Fear isn't in charge here when we believe the Word of God. That doesn't mean that we have no fears, but that we don't let fears "rule the roost." The Word of God is the biblical corrective for not going forward. Jeremiah heard the Word: "Do not be afraid . . . I will protect you." The New Testament puts it this way: "Fear not, little flock (Luke 12:32)." "Fear not, daughter of Zion (John 12:15)." At the empty tomb the angel said to the frightened women: "Do not be afraid (Matthew 28:5, RSV)."

As he departed this earth, Jesus promised "Lo I am with you always, to the close of the age (Matthew 28:20)."

Fear isn't in charge here when we believe the promise: "I will protect you . . . (Jeremiah 1:8, TEV)." Fear isn't in charge here when we believe Jesus' promise, "Lo I am with you always . . ."

Fear isn't in charge here, so we can minister because God calls us in baptism, gives us gifts for serving others and keeps his promise not to desert us!

Epiphany 5
Isaiah 6:1-8

Vision For Mission

There are many wonderful passages in the book of Isaiah, but none lovelier than this gem — the call of Isaiah in the temple of God. This text is lovely and bright in spite of dark elements of sin and unworthiness, because the light of God calling is not overcome by the darkness into which it comes. The light overcomes the darkness. The mission of Isaiah is to represent God. The mission of the Church of Jesus Christ is the same. That mission begins with vision.

Vision

Isaiah's vision includes self insight and a call to serve God's purposes in spite of human limitations. Isaiah sees his own uncleanness, "Woe is me! For I am lost." This sense of being lost in the presence of God is a sign of the true calling of this man of God. Martin Luther put it this way: "It is God's nature to create out of nothing. Unless you are nothing, God cannot make anything out of you." Isaiah sensed that he was nothing, that he was lost.

Have you ever gotten lost? I was lost when I was a child. It was at a big sports show in a bit amphitheater in Chicago. I think I was six or seven years old. Somehow I wandered away from my parents. It was scary with all that noise and all those people. I looked here, there and everywhere. Finally, over the loud speaker a big booming voice said, "If you are a little boy named Ron Lavin, please identify yourself and stand still so that your father can find you."

At about that same time in my life I nearly drowned. Our family was swimming at a big lake. I was playing at water's edge. The warning had been sounded, "Don't go into deep water." My parents glanced away for a moment and I was gone. They couldn't see me. Fortunately, a friend, Ann Orton, was there and she saw what happened. She dove in the dark water approximately where she saw me go under, found me and brought me to shore. I don't remember the details, but my parents always referred to Ann as the one who saved my life.

In both childhood experiences of being lost the chief ingredient was disorientation. Disorientation is what Isaiah must have felt too, but not because of unfamiliar places or a near drowning accident. He was disoriented by seeing a vision of God and his angels. In such heavenly company, Isaiah did not know where he was or who he was. He felt lost. He also felt unclean.

Isn't it strange how often a positive reorientation of our lives starts with a recognition of limitation. All of our resources disappear. All of our strength fades. We don't know where to turn or what to do. This often happens in serious illness, when divorce comes, when death takes a loved one or at critical times in the lives of alcoholics or drug users. Isaiah began his reorientation by confessing uncleanness in himself and all the people around him. "I am a man of unclean lips and I dwell in the midst of a people of unclean lips . . .," he said. We are all "undone . . ." We have all stepped over the line of sanity into insane thinking, acting or speaking. Perhaps our preconceptions were punctured, our illusions destroyed, our foundations shaken.

Paul Tillich, the theologian, calls this recognition of limitations "the shaking of the foundations." Tillich says, " 'The earth is split in pieces' is not merely a poetic metaphor for us, but a hard reality. That is the religious meaning of the age into which we have entered." He says that man has been given the power to destroy himself and modern man seems to be bent on using that power for self destruction. The threat of nuclear war and its catastrophic consequences is a shaking of foundations for many. Forgetting God and setting himself up as God, modern man brings despair and self destruction.

Tillich puts it this way:

> *When he (man) has rested complacently on his cultural creativity, or on his technical progress, on his political institutions or on his religious systems, he has been thrown into disintegration and chaos; all the foundations of his personal, natural and cultural life have been shaken. As long as there has been human history, this is what has happened; in our period it has happened on a larger scale than ever before.*

Now with that kind of analysis of our times, place yourself in the temple and experience with Isaiah the call to minister in the name of God. This call includes a vision of hot coals being placed on Isaiah's mouth. The meaning here is two-fold. Isaiah must be cleansed and he must speak with pure zeal for the Lord.

Isaiah is a man of his times. He, too, has fallen into idolatrous disloyalty to the Lord. He, too, is unclean. He, too, must repent. He, too, is sick and must be made well. The symbol of Isaiah's need for cleansing is the burning of his lips as a healing process. This burning is also a promise or proleptic of things to come. Isaiah will henceforth speak for God.

Zeal for God and God's ways will not be well received by the people of God. The people are satisfied. They don't want to change. They don't want to repent. Most human beings will not be receptive to the prophetic message that the very foundations of life are shaking. People caught in illusions deny their condition. They live with illusions until it is too late. Therefore, nothing less than persistence and zeal for the Lord will be necessary when one speaks for God. The burning of Isaiah's lips means prophetic proclamation and the call to repentance to a self-satisfied people.

The vision of Isaiah means seeing and hearing: seeing beyond which he beholds and hearing the Word of God about the noises of a materialistic world. The call of Isaiah includes voices as well as vision.

Voices

Angelic voices and the voice of the Lord are heard by the prophet. The angels said, "Behold, this (hot coal) has touched your lips, your guilt is taken away, and your sin forgiven."

Voices of forgiveness precede the voice of commission. God gives us something before he expects us to do something. The gift of renewal precedes responsibility for Isaiah and us. God never asks us to do anything without first equipping us to do it. Our real sense of inadequacy is overcome by God's greater adequacy. This story of Isaiah's call provides us with the biblical corrective for humanistic self-affirmation, distorted professionalism in ministry, and mixed priorities.

In our time there is a lot of talk about self-affirmation. We are told to believe in ourselves and love ourselves and forgive ourselves, but all too often the God factor is missing. Many human beings today try to have the benefits of forgiveness and renewal without a relationship with God. The New Age movement, for example, is based on self-fulfillment, but beneath the veneer there is little more than self-centeredness based on self-deification. All man-made religion is self-centered. The biblical corrective in Isaiah is that the living God must forgive and renew or we remain in our sins with only an illusion of forgiveness. The danger of humanistic affirmation looms large in our day.

The danger of professionalism in ministry also looms large. Ordained pastors insisting that they be treated like "other professionals" in compensation, respect, limits on their time, and their pension benefits have missed the point of the call. In other words, many ordained clergypersons see themselves primarily as professionals instead of called servants.

In the Evangelical Lutheran Church in America we have professional leaders' committees, conferences for professional leaders and a Division For Professional Leadership. All of this is well and good. In a certain sense, pastors are professionals. But that is secondary. Primarily, pastors are called ministers, servants of the gospel. Isaiah, chapter six, is a reminder to pastors and congregations alike that the call to serve is more important than any status as professionals. In other words, the call to mission is a matter of the highest priorities for clergypersons. That priority is not just for the ordained. That priority of the call to missions is for all Christians.

Is God's mission foremost in our lives? Are we more concerned with making money than saving souls? Are we really concerned about our lost brothers and sisters? Are we discovering the gifts of God for the service of God and thus discovering the will of God for our lives? Do we see our jobs as Christian vocations which afford us opportunities to witness? Do we have a giving spirit? Are we all listening for God's call? Is all that we do evaluated around the question, "Is it for God's glory?"

Pastors and laypersons are called by God to proclaim the Word of God, to the glory of God, to win people to God and his church, and to serve people in the church and the world selflessly like Jesus Christ did. Isaiah, chapter six, is the biblical corrective for a church and people easily led off center. We need to be reminded of the call of God to center life on God, his will and his glory.

The question of Isaiah 6:8 is the God question addressed to all of us to set the mission of God above everything else in life. "Whom shall I send as a messenger to my people? Who will go?"

Isaiah said, "Here I am. Send me."

What do you say?

Epiphany 6
Jeremiah 17:5-10

Trusting In The Lord

Recently I awoke from a dream with a start. I didn't know where I was or what was happening. I didn't even know who I was. I had fallen asleep in an armchair in the family room. That was quite an awakening to reality.

Some time ago, I had left a message at the desk of a hotel where I was staying. I wanted to get up at 6 a.m. so that I wouldn't miss an important meeting. The phone rang and a very pleasant voice on the other side said, "Mr. Lavin, this is your wake up call." Startled, I jumped out of bed, asking the question out loud, "What am I supposed to do?" Wake up calls are like that. They face us with reality, sometimes before we think we are ready.

Jeremiah was trying to wake up the people of his day to the reality of God. They were asleep to the reality of God; filled with illusions about themselves and religion. They accused Jeremiah of being a dreamer, but they were the ones who were out of touch with reality. Jeremiah said that they were cursed because they trusted in human potential and neglected the potential of the living Lord.

Jeremiah was a God-driven man who spoke fearlessly about the moral laxity and social ills of the nation and warned of disasters. Faith in Yahweh instead of idols is the call of Jeremiah. Faith means trust. Trust in Yahweh, instead of trust in false gods or mortal man, is Jeremiah's theme.

Trust In Humankind

Specifically, the people of God of Jeremiah's day had put their trust in idols, in kings, in treaties and in human effort to achieve pleasurable goals. Man, God's two-footed handiwork, had worked himself into the center where Yahweh alone belongs. Humankind in the middle was the problem. Jeremiah predicted that this arrangement of man in the middle would never work.

Can a stunted plant in the desert survive with no life-giving water? Can a desert tree survive without life-giving water? Neither can you survive if you put yourself in first place where you do not have the water of life, says the Lord. The human heart is deceitful. It fools us. We give our love to those things which will only hurt us. We are lured into self-centered and self-defeating patterns of trusting those things which do not deliver happiness. We turn from the Lord who alone produces true life, who alone belongs in first place. Human beings are eccentric, off center. That's the heart of sin. The result of this radical dislocation of authority is hopelessness. "The beast is easily deceived," Jeremiah said. The human problem of the dislocation of the authority in the deceitful human heart is as modern as the morning newspaper.

In the early 1900s, a parish pastor in Switzerland by the name of Karl reflected the spirit of his times which was human achievement. Like so many other clergymen of liberal persuasion, Karl saw the kingdom of God in human terms. He believed that political changes for the common man could usher in the kingdom of God. He was a socialist politically and a liberal theologically. He was also a scholar who began research on a commentary on the book of Romans.

In 1919, Karl published his commentary on Romans. In this commentary, he broke from anthropocentric and cultural Christianity of the European liberals of his day. Paul's words in Romans led Karl Barth back to a God-centered Christianity and ushered in a movement called neo-orthodoxy. Barth said, "The main problem with (theological) liberalism is that man is the center, and measure and goal of all things." One of his biographers puts it this way: "Liberals began with Christian experience. Barth begins with objective activity of God in revelation." Thereafter, Barth saw the kingdom of God in terms of God's sovereign reign; not humankind's efforts. Thus

Barth echoes Jeremiah: "Blessed is the man who trusts in the Lord."

At a more practical level, John was a materialist. He had caught the spirit of his time which was "Take care of number one." He believed what authors and lecturers in the 1970s were telling him about self-fulfillment. "If you can't take care of yourself first, nobody will take care of you," he said. He was successful in business, rich and owned so many things (later he called them "adult toys"), that he could not keep track of them. He was a part of the instant-gratification "Me Generation." His world fell apart when his wife left him because of his alcoholism and drug habits. John began what he later called "a long journey home" by hitting rock bottom, going to Alcoholics Anonymous and eventually returning to his church and his faith in Jesus Christ as Lord.

As a materialist, John had gone to church with his family on holidays, but he always thought of church as "a place for weaklings." Now that he could not get himself out of his own hands, realizing that he was ruled by alcohol, John submitted to Christ as Lord and Savior and started a new life. Thus John echoes Jeremiah's corrective, "Cursed is the man who trusts in man." He also reflects Jeremiah's admonition, "Blessed is the man who trusts in the Lord."

Trust In Our Lord

Trusting God is the one thing needful, and the hardest thing of all. Trusting is the one thing needful because faith means trust and the Bible teaches that only faith saves us. "By faith you are saved through grace and this is not your own doing lest anyone should boast (Ephesians 2:8)."

Paul, who wrote these words, also wrote, "The gospel is the power of God unto salvation for all who believe (Romans 1:16)." The gospel is the good news that we can trust God in Jesus Christ, our Savior and our Lord. Paul had trusted his own religion and his own opinions prior to his conversion.

Saul had a man-made religion before he became Paul of the Christ-centered faith.

Man-made religion is upward and inward. Christ centered religion is downward and outward. The difference is immense. It is the difference between idolatry and true faith. It is the difference between being cursed and blessed, to put it in Jeremiah's words. The blessed ones trust God instead of self.

Trusting God is not easy. It is hard for Paul, Karl and John. It is hard for all of us to trust the Lord. When people have disappointed us, we find it hard to trust God.

At a practical level, a woman, let's call her Dee, found it almost impossible to trust God. As a little girl she had experienced incest, forced sex with her father. Now as an adult she was having trouble trusting Christ as Lord and Savior. A Christian counselor helped her overcome her background and start a new life as a Christian. She felt dirty. He helped her see that she was loved by God. She felt trapped in a dysfunctional family. He helped her to be a functional and integrated adult through Christ. "That is a blessed state," she said. "It was like waking up to a reality, the reality of God, whom I now confess as my heavenly Father." Dee got her wake-up call and answered it positively.

We wake up to reality as we trust in Christ. We know who we are and where we are when we discover whose we are.

Thanks, Jeremiah. We needed that!

Epiphany 7
Genesis 45:1-11, 15
Faithful To The Lord

There are many plots, sub-plots and themes in the Old Testament story of Joseph. The plots and sub-plots are intriguing background for the theme of faithfulness and forgiveness. The main plot is that God is faithfully at work in this holy family. The sub-plots can be misleading.

Family Conflict, Temptation And Dreams

For example, there is a sub-plot of family conflict between the 11 sons of Jacob or Israel, as he is later called. Son number 11 is Joseph. (Son number 12, Benjamin, came along later in life.) From Jacob's 12 boys the 12 tribes of Israel are formed. The conflict arises because Joseph is the favored son of Jacob. We don't know why, but we do know that Joseph was his father's pride and joy. Conflict and intrigue come when a father plays favorites. Joseph is the favorite son. The plot thickens as we see that Joseph is also a dreamer with obnoxious overconfidence. One of Joseph's favorite dreams, and his brothers' least favorite themes, had his brothers bowing down before him. Soon thereafter, the brothers entered into a conspiracy to kill Joseph. They changed their plans and sold Joseph to Egyptian traders instead. They then told their father that Joseph was dead, using Joseph's blood-soaked coat of many colors as evidence of the death. Family conflict is an interesting sub-plot which later sets up the theme of faithfulness.

Another interesting sub-plot includes Potiphar, captain of the king's personal bodyguards, and his wife. Joseph rose to a place of honor and responsibility in Potiphar's household. Potiphar's wife was sexually attracted to Joseph, but Joseph steadfastly refused her advances. One day when she was even more direct in her sexual overtures than usual, Joseph plainly told her "No" and fled from her presence. She was clinging to his robes as he departed. The robe came loose as Joseph fled. Bitter and resentful at being turned down, Potiphar's wife accused Joseph of trying to rape her. That accusation resulted in Joseph's imprisonment. The sexual temptation and the prison period are sub-plots in this story of faithfulness.

Dreams are another interesting sub-theme in the story of Joseph. While in his homeland, Joseph's dream of his superiority caused him no little conflict in his family. While in Egypt, and in prison, Joseph's interpretation of the dreams of the chief baker and the chief butler of the king of Egypt led to his release from prison where the three had been thrown for various offenses.

We pick up the story with the king having a recurring dream which no one could interpret. The chief butler, now restored to his proper place, told the king about Joseph's accuracy in interpreting dreams which he had observed when they were both in prison. The dream of the king was interpreted by Joseph to mean seven years of plenty and seven years of famine. Joseph became governor over the granaries of Egypt with that interpretation, storing up goods during the years of plenty.

It is good that we review the Old Testament story of Joseph. Many people don't know the story; others have forgotten the details. Many people are confused about the Old Testament, like the little Sunday school student who, when asked about her favorite Old Testament stories, said: "Noah's wife and Lot's wife." "Can you summarize them for me?" asked the Sunday school teacher. "Sure," said the little girl, "Noah's wife was Joan of Arc and Lot's wife was a pillar of salt by day and a ball of fire by night."

It's good that we study the Old Testament story of Joseph to get the historical details straight, but there is much more than history here. The Word of God is here for us if we have the eyes to see it and the ears to hear it. That Word has to do with faithfulness.

As interesting as the conspiracy of his brothers, the temptation of Potiphar's wife and the interpretation of dreams may be, the story of Joseph is best understood under the theme "faithfulness." Joseph was faithful to his family. In our time when family disloyalties run rampant, that is a Word in season. Joseph was faithful to God through many adversities which would have been the undoing of a lesser man. In our day a time of fickle faith, that is a well-timed reminder. As evidence of this faithfulness, Joseph gave a new interpretation on reality and started a new life for himself and his enemies through forgiveness.

A New Interpretation Of Reality

We pick up the story in chapter 45 verse one. After years of separation, Joseph confronts his brothers with the reality of who he is. In a world-wide famine, the brothers have come to Egypt for food. Joseph, the governor of Egypt in charge of food distribution, has them right where we think he wants them. They had been jealous and conniving. They had sold their own flesh and blood to traders. Now Joseph has a chance to get even. Revenge, that major theme, not only of novels but of life itself, looms large at the poignant moment of confrontation when Joseph reveals his identity. But Joseph puts a new interpretation on the reality of the betrayal, the conspiracy and the brotherly intrigue.

"God, not you, sent me here to Egypt," Joseph says to his stunned brothers. "God sent me here ahead of you to preserve your lives . . . God sent me here to keep you and your families alive . . . God made me a counselor to Pharaoh and a manager of the entire nation, a ruler of all the land of Egypt." Viewing events in the light of faith, Joseph sees them from a higher perspective. "You meant this for evil, but God meant it for good," he said. This is a higher view of reality than we expect. Joseph's behavior is a revelation.

Being faithful to God means having this higher view of reality. God works good even in evil circumstances. God is faithful to us, even when life seems to be saying that God has forsaken us. Trying to be truthful, Joseph was sold by his brothers. Trying to be moral and resist temptation, Joseph was thrown into prison as an innocent victim of a plotting and scheming woman. Trying to be a man of faith, Joseph spent years behind bars for a crime he did not commit. Bitterness is generally made of such ingredients. Resentment builds in the human heart under such a devious set of circumstances. "Where was God when I needed him?" Joseph might have said. Instead, Joseph saw the hand of God working through the bad times as well as the good. Joseph remained faithful through it all.

What difference does the story of Joseph make to us? This story is an invitation to view reality from a higher point of view and remain faithful to God when life turns sour.

Paul, the apostle, describes faithfulness in spite of adversity this way: ". . . In everything God works for good with those who love him, who are called according to his purpose (Romans 8:28)." "We are afflicted in every way, but not crushed; perplexed, but not driven to despair; persecuted, but not forsaken; struck down, but not destroyed (2 Corinthians 4:8-9)."

Charles Swindoll puts it like this:

> *Nothing touches me that has not passed through the hands of my heavenly Father. Nothing. Everything I endure is designed to prepare me for serving others more effectively. Everything.*

Faithfulness to the Lord means having this higher perspective. Faithfulness also means being willing to forgive.

New Life Through Forgiveness

Joseph forgave his brothers because they needed it. He forgave them before they asked for it. He forgave them when they did not deserve it. In being faithful to God, Joseph acted toward his brothers like God acts toward his children, with forgiveness. The brothers all wept when they realized who Joseph was and what he was doing.

Forgiveness is the stuff out of which faithfulness is made. Forgiveness is God's orientation toward his children. Forgiveness is the ingredient out of which new life comes. When we are willing to forgive, we are acting like Jesus, who said, "Father, forgive them for they know not what they do."

St. Francis of Assisi embodied much of the teaching of Jesus. The prayer of St. Francis is a classic example of the meaning of forgiveness in real life. Joseph lived out this prayer long before it was written. In this prayer we, too, are challenged to be faithful by being willing to forgive.

Lord, make me an instrument of
 your peace.
Where there is hatred,
 let me sow love.
Where there is injury,
 pardon.
Where there is doubting,
 let me bring your faith.
Where there is despair,
 let me bring your hope.
Where there is darkness,
 your light.
Where there is sadness,
 let me bring your joy.
Grant that I might not so much seek to be consoled
 as to console;
To be understood
 as to understand;
Not so much to be loved
 as to love another.
For it is in giving that we now receive;
 It is in pardoning that we are now pardoned,
And it is in dying that we are born again.

God's plot is to use the story of Joseph and his family to show us what faithfulness means.

Epiphany 8
Isaiah 55:10-13

Believing The Living Word

There are few things in life which you can count on, but you can count on these two: the Word of God goes forth, and the Word of God does not return empty.

The rain falls to the earth and gives life to flowers, plants and trees before it returns to God who sent it. Water means life. The Word of God is like that water. In the Word and the water we have the possibility of new life beginning. Not every plant grows; not every human being is connected by the Word. But the life is there for the taking.

Perhaps you have some friend or relative for whom you have prayed for a long time. At times it seems like a hopeless cause. You pray and pray for years and nothing seems to change. The object of your affection, a son, a daughter, a wife or husband, a father or mother, just won't give in and believe in God. Instead, stunted and turned in on self, these loved ones go on living as materialists or practical atheists. They live as secular people, as if there is no God. Your heart is broken. You witness, talk and pray, seemingly to no avail. Here in today's Word there is hope, "My Word goes forth . . . it shall not return to me empty."

The Word Goes Forth

The Word of God in the Old Testament means a spoken utterance about God. The concept of the Word comes from the Hebrew word *dabar*. The term "the Word of the Lord" occurs 400 times in the Old Testament and means any communication from God to man. It generally means the word of a prophet who speaks for God. Here in Isaiah 55 we hear that as the Word of the Lord is promulgated or proclaimed, it is like rain or snow. It goes forth and prospers, bringing new life. Some believe — not all, but some. Those who believe have eternal life as a blessing.

The Word of God in the New Testament is the translation of one of two Greek nouns, *logos* and *rhema*, which both come from verb roots which mean "to say." The Word is what God says. Logos is used 300 times; rhema, 70 times. Perhaps the most familiar passage about the Word is the opening passage of the Gospel of John.

> *In the beginning was the Word, and the Word was with God, and the Word was God. He was in the beginning with God; all things were made through him, and without him was not anything made that was made. In him was life, and the life was the light of men. The light shines in the darkness, and the darkness has not overcome it . . . And the Word became flesh and dwelt among us, full of grace and truth; we have beheld his glory, glory as of the only Son from the Father. (John bore witness to him, and cried, "This was he of whom I said, 'He who comes after me ranks before me, for he was before me.' ") And from his fullness have we all received grace upon grace.*   — John 1:1-16, RSV

In other words, in the New Testament the primary affirmation is that the Word goes forth in the person of Jesus Christ. In Jesus the Word of God is given flesh. We who believe in Jesus, the incarnate Word, are given new life, eternal life, receiving "grace upon grace." In Jesus, the Word is seen, heard and believed. In Jesus, the Word, we are blessed.

The Word also goes forth in the written form of the Bible. The early Christians were told not to leave the Word of God (Acts 6:2), which means that they were urged to read the Scriptures regularly. They were also urged to handle the written Word without deceit (2 Corinthians 4:2). The written Word is like a helmet of salvation (Ephesians 6:17). The written Word protects the brain and makes our thoughts whole.

The third form of the Word in the New Testament is the preached Word, the proclamation of the gospel of salvation in Jesus Christ. In Acts 13:44 we hear about the preaching of the gospel, ". . . Almost the whole city was gathered together to hear the Word of God." The gospel message was preached in Antioch by Paul and Barnabas (Also see Luke 5:1; 1 Thessalonians 1:8 and 2 Thessalonians 3:1). In other words, the Word goes forth in the form of preaching the Gospel of Christ. Preaching in the New Testament is more than just the preaching of apostles and pastors in the context of worship services. In the New Testament, preaching is the witness and sharing of all the people of God.

Paul advises his young protege, Timothy, that until Christ returns: "Preach the Word; be ready in season and out of season; reprove, rebuke, exhort without great patience and instruction (2 Timothy 4:2)." Why preach? Because God uses preaching to bring people to faith.

This Word Does Not Return Empty

The specific context for the Old Testament promise in Isaiah 55 is the Word spoken through the prophets of God. When the prophets spoke the Word of God, some people believed. In the New Testament we have the same assurance of the Word reaching peoples' hearts in the person of Jesus Christ, the Scriptures and the preaching of the gospel. Not all believe, but the Word goes forth and always some believe and live.

Jesus Christ gives us unmerited grace upon grace. Some people resist that freely given grace for years, and then one day the barrier is broken. Jesus gets through. All the witnessing and example of Christians which seem to have been in vain, one day bear fruit. The Word Jesus Christ scores a victory over sin, death and the demonic forces which try to combine to keep people from God. The Word wins out over great odds.

For example, recently the Word got through to a man named Harry. After 76 years of life turned in on self, Harry finally said, "Yes" to Jesus Christ. Luther said we are curved in on the self *(en curvitas en se)* until we are turned to Christ. When Christ wins us over, our center changes from self to God. The Word, like water, brings nourishment and life.

Romano Guardini, a Roman Catholic bishop, puts it this way: "Until we make the transposition to Christ we will fight, found and form this or that . . . without affecting the constantly flowing sands of time for more than an instant." The Word, when appropriated, changes all that. For Harry this transposition happened recently in baptism.

The Word does not return empty. Bible verses by the hundreds had been read to Harry, all with no apparent effect. I read many passages from Scripture to him when he was taken down with a stroke about a year and a half before he was baptized. The words seemed like so much water off a duck's back. But the Word of God as it was shared was like so many seeds planted in Harry's life. On Wednesday, June 14, 1989, Harry was baptized. The plant, watered all these years, finally bloomed.

The Bible passages had been resisted. The Word seemed ineffective, but was actually working quietly and powerfully in Harry's heart. Charles Spurgeon was once asked how he would defend the Bible. "Defend it?" he asked. "Would you defend a lion? The Scripture does not need to be defended. Just set it free. It will defend itself." That happened to Harry. Words of Scripture graced his baptism. The Word, as Scripture, was set free to defend itself and create a new life. The preached Word was also effective in Harry's life.

The preached Word is not just the Sunday sermons by pastors but the witnessing to Christ by many people in many ways. Occasionally sermons were heard, but in Harry's case he just yawned. Witnessing to Christ seemed to bear no fruit. Many Christians witnessed to Harry and prayed for him, including his wife who was a devout Christian and his grandchildren who talked to him about God. None of it seemed to help. But God has made a promise, "My Word shall not return to me empty." The witness of hundreds of people came to fruition on June 14, 1989. Christ was confessed as Lord and Savior. Harry was baptized.

We sometimes wondered whether all the effort was in vain. In Harry's life the Word did not seem to bring life. Who would have guessed that the Word would bring forth life the very weekend that I preached on this text? This sermon on Isaiah 55:10-13 was outlined about six months before it was preached. On the morning of June 14, a sermon manuscript on this text was begun. In relationship to Harry, the Word seemed untrue that morning. As I wrote the sermon on this text I thought, "If the Word does not return empty after visiting the earth, then why is Harry still outside the church? Will he ever find new life in Christ?" That was the morning of June 14, 1989. On the evening of June 14, I received a phone call from Chicago saying: "We have some good news for you," Harry said. "Today I was baptized."

It is very good for me to share this good news with you. It is good to write it down. It is good to include it in this chapter about the Word not returning empty. When Harry was baptized, it was an answer to hundreds and hundreds of prayers for more than 33 years. As I have preached and lectured around the country, I always ask the groups of people to pray for Harry. "Wing your prayers toward Chicago, Illinois," I requested. "We don't know what prayer is, only that it is. We don't know how prayer works, only that it works. Pray for Harry's conversion and baptism before he dies," I said. "I love him. I want him to find peace through Jesus Christ before he dies."

Water came down from heaven. Some of it fell into Lake Michigan and became a part of the watering system of Chicago. Some of it was put into a bowl and used for Harry's baptism on June 14. It thus became holy water, sacramental water. That water has now returned to the heavens from which it came, having touched a human being in a sacramental way.

Harry was 75 years old when he almost died of a stroke in 1988. At this writing, he is still bedridden. But things are different now. Harry is baptized. He belongs to God. He is getting prepared for the final chapter of his life. He is prepared to meet his Maker. The living Word has gotten through and returns to heaven having done its job — preparing someone for eternity.

The Word of God is alive and working. The Word became flesh and dwelt among us full of grace and truth. "Grace upon grace" was experienced in the water of baptism. I am a very happy man. I am a happy son. Harry is my father.

The Transfiguration Of Our Lord
Exodus 34:29-35

Transformed For The Great Awakening

Moses experienced the presence of the living God. Therein he was transformed. His face shone. He smiled broadly. Light shone round about him. Everyone noticed the difference. There was a radiance about Moses after he had talked with God. In Hebrew this radiance is called *shekinah* or Divine Presence.

The question raised by our text is the question of radiance. Are we going to let our lights so shine before others that they will be led to faith? The question is not, "How much light do you have?" but "Will we let it shine?" The child's song about light raises the question simply but beautifully:

> *This little light of mine*
> *I'm going to let it shine*
> *Let it shine, Let it shine, Let it shine.*

Before we look more closely at the implications of letting our lights shine before other people, let us look at Moses' radiance and the radiance of our Lord Jesus Christ.

Moses And Jesus

Why did Moses smile so broadly and shine so brightly? He had been in the presence of God. He had received the ten commandments, a Law by which the people could live. Moses had talked with God. His face was aglow (Exodus 24:35, LB) because he had been with the God of glory. Moses had experienced the glory of God. Now that glory was a part of him.

The root word for glory can mean either horns or light. Some artists of the middle ages painted Moses with horns on his head. Michelangelo picked up the mistake in his famous statue of Moses. Instead of a halo, Michelangelo gave Moses horns. Light, not horns, emanated from Moses' head.

The angelic glow of Moses' face was so mysterious that Moses had to cover his face as he talked with the people. He had fasted for 40 days and nights while on the mountain with God. Now as he re-entered ordinary life, Moses shone with God's glory. This shining was even more apparent in Jesus' transfiguration as recorded in Matthew 17:1-8, Mark 9:2-13 and Luke 9:28-36.

> *And after six days Jesus took with him Peter and James and John his brother, and led them up a high mountain apart. And he was transfigured before them, and his face shone like the sun, and his garments became white as light. And behold, there appeared to them Moses and Elijah, talking with him. And Peter said to Jesus, "Lord, it is well that we are here; and if you wish, I will make three booths here, one for you and one for Moses and one for Elijah." He was still speaking, when lo, a bright cloud overshadowed them, and a voice from the cloud said, "This is my beloved Son, with whom I am well pleased; listen to him." When the disciples heard this, they fell on their faces and were filled with awe. But Jesus came and touched them, saying, "Rise, and have no fear." And when they lifted up their eyes, they saw no one but Jesus only.* — Matthew 17:1-8, RSV

In this story of Jesus' transfiguration we have the key to transformation: "They saw Jesus only." In its original context this phrase meant that Moses (standing for the Law) and Elijah (standing for the prophets) had disappeared. Peter, James and John saw only Jesus. They saw him in all his glory. These three apostles were transformed because all distractions were removed. For us, this focus on Jesus only with no distractions also results in transformation.

We Have This Treasure Of Divine Light

In 2 Corinthians chapters 3 and 4, Paul picks up the theme of the light of Christ shining through common Christians. The Living Bible paraphrase of 2 Corinthians 3:12-18 is enlightening.

> *Since we know that this new glory will never go away, we can preach with great boldness, and not as Moses did, who put a veil over his face so that the Israelites could not see the glory fade away. Not only Moses' face was veiled, but his people's minds and understanding were veiled and blinded, too . . . This veil of misunderstanding can be removed only by believing in Christ. Yes, even today when they read Moses' writings their hearts are blind and they think that obeying the Ten Commandments is the way to be saved. But whenever anyone turns to the Lord from his sins, then the veil is taken away. The Lord is the Spirit who gives them life, and where he is there is freedom (from trying to be saved by keeping the Laws of God). But we Christians have no veil over our faces; we can be mirrors that brightly reflect the glory of the Lord. And as the Spirit of the Lord works within us, we become more and more like him.*

We are mirrors. That's it. That's the missing ingredient in most of our churches. That's the missing element in much of our preaching. That's what is missing in many church members' lives. Christ is the light of the world. We are mirrors. All we have to do is focus on Jesus and reflect that light.

What is the purpose of the church? To reflect the glory of Christ, our Lord. Get that purpose clear and things have a way of falling into place. Miss that purpose and many good things may be done, but the radiance will be missing.

Paul develops this focus on Christ to its horizons and also speaks of our human limitations in 2 Corinthians, chapter four:

> *Even if this gospel is veiled, it is veiled only to those who are perishing.* (v. 3)

For what we preach is not ourselves, but Jesus Christ as Lord, with ourselves as your servants for Jesus' sake.
(v. 5)

This reflection in a mirror is not perfect as Paul explains in verse 7:

But we have this treasure (of Christ) in earthen vessels, to show that the transcendent power belongs to God, and not to us.

In other words, we are not perfect instruments for transmitting divine light to the world. But we don't have to be perfect! We just need to reflect Christ's glory. There is still darkness in those who convey the light of God, but that should not be an inhibiting factor in letting the light of God shine through us. Our lights are little compared to the light of Moses and Jesus, but there is no reason to hide the light under a bushel basket. The container for this treasure of splendor is frail flesh, but that doesn't matter. We don't focus on the pottery holding this treasure, but on the treasure itself. Jesus is that light.

Since Jesus Christ has come and since he is the light which enlightens every man, we can reflect that light like a mirror. That light of Christ lightens the darkness of this world. "In him (Jesus) was life and that life was the light of men. The light shines in the darkness and the darkness has not overcome it (John 1:4-5, RSV)."

This light changes everyone it touches. Therefore we are called to reflect this light as God's transformed people. John puts it this way:

The true light that enlightens every man was coming into the world. He was in the world, and the world was made through him, yet the world knew him not. He came to his own home, and his own people received him not. But to all who received him, who believed in his name, he gave power to become the children of God; who were born not of blood, nor of the will of the flesh, nor of the will of man, but of God.
— John 1:9-12, RSV

Let me put it another way. We Christians have been given a gift of light to see beyond what we behold. We have glimpses of the kingdom of God. Those glimpses need to be shared!

For now we see in a mirror dimly, but then face to face. Now I know in part; then I shall understand fully, even as I have been fully understood.
— 1 Corinthians 13:12, RSV)

Let me say it again, this time using Paul's words in Romans 12:2:

Do not be conformed to this world but be transformed by the renewal of your mind, that you may prove what is the will of God, what is good and acceptable and perfect.

Transformed people — that's what is needed for our day — transformed people who let their lights shine until the second coming of Christ. Radiant smiles and glowing reports of what God has done in Christ and continues to do in the Holy Spirit — that's what transformed Christian people need to share, thus sharing with others the best preview of the coming attraction of God's reign.

Let me say it one last time, this time through two children's stories and a children's song. A little girl who loved her grandmother very much and saw the light of Christ in what her grandmother did and said observed: "Grandma must sleep in heaven with the Lord because she is so happy at breakfast."

Danny, a 12-year-old paper boy in Las Vegas, Nevada, was delivering papers one day when the man at the door said, "I don't want a paper. I don't need a paper. My wife is dying of cancer." The man slammed the door in Danny's face as Danny said, "Would you like my pastor to call?" Danny, a confirmation student, told the pastor about what happened. "There isn't much we can do," the pastor said. "Pastor, would you go see him?" Danny asked directly. The pastor agreed to try. All that week the busy pastor put off making the call, but he knew that he had to face Danny at confirmation class the next week.

Finally, the pastor visited the home. "Your paper boy, Danny, told me that your wife has cancer," the pastor said to the man at the door. "I'm here to offer my help. I'm a Lutheran pastor." The man at the door looked angry. "I don't know what a Lutheran is and I don't know what a pastor is," he said. He started to slam the door. The pastor put his calling card in the man's hand, saying "Call me if you need me."

Some weeks later the phone rang. "We'd like you to come to the home," the man said. "If you are a friend of Danny's, maybe you can help." The woman was dying of cancer. She was hooked up to an oxygen machine. The atmosphere in the house was bleak. "I've never seen the inside of a church," she said, "but I've heard a rumor that you Christians take 'bread and wine and believe that God is present.' I need God's presence. Can you help me?"

Soon thereafter, Danny's pastor baptized the woman and gave her the bread and wine of the presence. The whole room was lit up by the smile on the woman's face. All this happened because of a boy named Danny, and his "little light."

The children's song says it beautifully:

This little light of mine
I'm going to let it shine.
Let it shine. Let it shine. Let it shine.

Don't let Satan blow it out.
I'm going to let it shine.
Don't let Satan blow it out.
I'm going to let it shine.
Let it shine. Let it shine. Let it shine.

Hide it under a bushel? No!
I'm going to let it shine.
Hide it under a bushel? No!
I'm going to let it shine.
Let it shine. Let it shine. Let it shine.

Let it shine till Jesus comes.
I'm going to let it shine.
Let it shine till Jesus comes.
I'm going to let it let it shine
Let it shine. Let it shine. Let it shine.

"Let it (your light) shine till Jesus comes" — that's the theme of this chapter. That's the theme of this book. Jesus is coming in what is called "the last days." When he comes ". . . every knee shall bow . . . and every tongue confess that Jesus is Lord to the glory of God the Father (Philippians 2:10-11)." In the meantime, the time between the creation and second coming of Christ, we have previews of coming attractions, one of which is that we know enough of Christ and what he does for people that we let "this little light of mine" shine until the end, the great awakening when ". . . the trumpets will sound, the dead will be raised imperishable and we shall be changed (1 Corinthians 15:52)." We are transformed in order to give previews of the coming attraction called "the great awakening."

www.ingramcontent.com/pod-product-compliance
Lightning Source LLC
Chambersburg PA
CBHW060845050426
42453CB00008B/838